NELSON
CENGAGE Learning

# Eco 1 Plus

## Activities for NCEA Economics Level One

Kelly Bigwood

Anne Younger

# Contents

| Pages 10–11 | = | Running reference to the related content in *Eco1 – Economics for NCEA Level One* textbook. |

ISBN: 9780170241946

# Consumer choices using demand

1    Define choice.

Page 8

_____

2    Sometimes our family or whanau help us to gain the things we want and so can be included in our means. Describe a situation where your family or whanau has helped you to satisfy a need or want.

_____

_____

_____

_____

3    a    Describe a recent situation where you were unable to get what you wanted because you did not have the means, in other words, the time or skills or money.

_____

     b    Identify the economic term we use to describe this problem.

_____

4    Think back to a time when you had to make a choice because of scarcity. For example, you were unable to buy both items you wanted so you had to make a choice.
     a    Describe the situation, including details of what options were available.

_____

_____

_____

     b    Identify the choice you made and explain why you made that choice.

_____

_____

_____

     c    Identify the next best option or alternative, that is, the option you missed out on.

_____

ISBN: 9780170241946

**5** Renee and Jon have saved $10 000 over the last few years, which they will use in one of the following ways:
- Going on a trip to Disneyland
- Starting a new small business
- Putting the $10 000 in the bank

**a** Explain whether the trip to Disneyland is a want or a need for Renee and Jon.

_____

_____

_____

**b** If Jon and Renee decided to go to Disneyland, explain one possible consequence of this decision.

_____

_____

_____

Page 9

**6** You have $20 and there are several things you want to do with it:
- A night at the movies
- Top-up your pre-paid cellphone
- Save it
- Download an album

You decide to top-up your cellphone. Identify three possible flow-on effects of your decision. In other words, what might happen as a result of your choice?

_____

_____

_____

_____

**7** Identify a possible opportunity cost for each of the following:

**a** Choosing to study Economics at university.

_____

**b** Choosing to spend a year overseas doing volunteer work.

_____

**c** Choosing to play netball every Saturday.

_____

**d** Choosing a vegetarian diet.

_____

**e** Going to a movie on Friday night.

_____

**f** Choosing a sugar free diet.

_____

**g** Buying a 12 month bus ticket to travel 2 km to school.

_____

ISBN: 9780170241946

Page 10–11

**8** Complete the table below. List four options for spending your free time this weekend. List at least two advantages and disadvantages of choosing each option. Answer the questions that follow.

| Option | Advantages | Disadvantages |
|---|---|---|
| 1 | | |
| 2 | | |
| 3 | | |
| 4 | | |

**a** After weighing up each advantage and disadvantage, rank the four options from best to worst.

_____

_____

_____

**b** Identify the option you have chosen and identify the opportunity cost (that is, the next best alternative).

_____

_____

**c** Describe a flow-on effect of your choice.

_____

_____

**d** Identify one possible way the decision could have a flow-on effect to another person or group.

_____

_____

**9** Austen works for an accountant, earning a salary with a net income of $2500 per fortnight. Her home needs a lot of renovating before she sells it. Austen has three options regarding the renovating: (1) She can renovate it herself on the weekends, but since that will take too long, she has decided to choose one of the other two options; (2) quit her job and renovate it herself, or (3) hire other people to renovate it for her.

**a** Identify the three options Austen has regarding the renovation of her home.

_____

_____

_____

**b** Austen chose to give up her job and renovate the house herself. She is pleased because she does not have to pay someone to do it for her. Explain to Austen the true cost of the choice she has made.

_____

_____

_____

**c** Describe one flow-on effect of the choice Austen has made.

_____

_____

**10** Use the words below to complete the diagram.

Limited        Time        Cost        Decision        Needs

Skills        Opportunity        Wants        Scarcity        Money

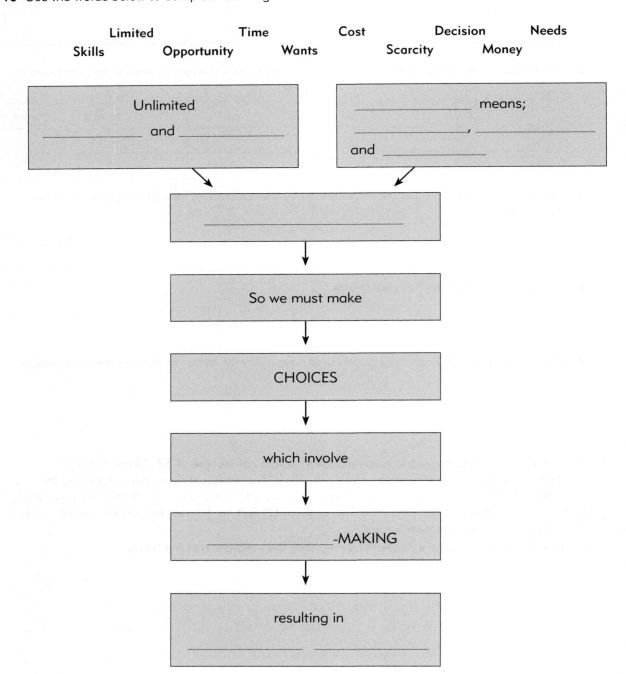

ISBN: 9780170241946

11 Meaghan describes herself as a 'Jack of all trades'. There are so many co-curricular activities she loves to be involved in; she plays netball for club and school, is learning the clarinet, is in Stage Challenge and 'Bring it On' at school and is involved in dancing and drama club outside of school. She really loves playing the clarinet, but just doesn't have enough time in the week to practise because of her other activities. Without practise, she will not be able to develop her skill and the teacher has told her that she needs to put the practise in or stop playing. The time has come for Meaghan to choose between the clarinet and dancing. Explain the economic problem that Meaghan is facing.

_____

_____

_____

_____

_____

_____

_____

_____

_____

_____

12 Define integrity.

Page 13

_____

13 Describe your cultural background or the culture that you identify with.

_____

_____

_____

14 Explain one way in which your cultural background has influenced your decision making.

_____

_____

15 A 30 second television advertisement during the US Super Bowl can cost several million dollars.
   a   Outline why firms would pay this much for a 30 second advertisement.

_____

_____

   b   Draw a conclusion about what this huge cost indicates about the impact that the media can have on consumer decision making.

_____

_____

ISBN: 9780170241946

**16** Melody has a part-time job as a youth worker at her local church and is also finishing her degree in design at university. She has several activities she likes to do on weekends; she has recently joined a club where they are committed to conservation and spends several weekends a month planting pohutukawa trees in areas where they are under threat. Melody also loves playing the drums, rehearsing in a band she has formed with her friends, and they are starting to get some paid gigs. Church and time with her boyfriend Andrew has to be fitted into her weekends too!

**a** Explain how weekend time is a limited resource for Melody. Use the terms scarcity, choice and opportunity cost in your answer.

_____

_____

_____

_____

_____

_____

_____

_____

_____

_____

_____

**b** Explain the way values might influence how Melody might choose to spend her time:

**i** If Melody values ecological sustainability.

_____

_____

_____

**ii** If Melody values financial stability.

_____

_____

_____

**c** Explain how a conflict might arise between the decisions in **b** above.

_____

_____

_____

**d** Explain how Melody might resolve the conflicts identified in **c** above.

_____

_____

ISBN: 9780170241946

17  Laura really loves *Smuggle* stationery. She is off to the shop to buy some erasers. At a normal price of $1.50 she would buy four erasers, however, when she arrives at the shop they are on special for half price. She decides to buy eight erasers. If the price had been $2.00, she could have bought two. Use this data to prepare a fully labelled demand schedule for Laura's monthly demand for *Smuggle* erasers.

Page 15

|  |  |
|---|---|
|  |  |
|  |  |
|  |  |
|  |  |

18  Hamish will buy 10 cups of coffee a week when the price is $3.00. He cuts back to eight cups a week if the price is $3.50, to six cups if the price is $4.00, and to five if the price is $4.50 – just one a day at work.

a   Create Hamish's Demand Schedule for Coffee per week

|  |  |
|---|---|
|  |  |
|  |  |
|  |  |
|  |  |

b   Explain the law of demand in the context of Hamish's demand for coffee.

19  Explain the difference between want and demand.

Page 17–19

20  Use the following demand schedule to construct a demand curve.

| Aroha's Monthly Demand for Movie Tickets ||
| Price ($) | Quantity demanded (tickets) |
|---|---|
| 7 | 5 |
| 8 | 4 |
| 9 | 3 |
| 10 | 2 |
| 11 | 1 |

**Aroha's Monthly Demand Curve for Movie Tickets**

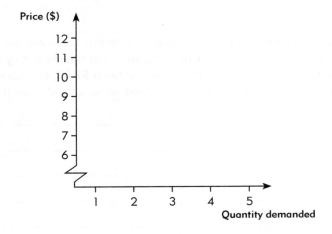

**21** Use the following demand curve graph to answer the questions below.

**Rao's Weekly Demand Curve for Cappuccinos**

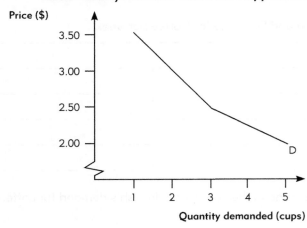

**a** Use Rao's demand curve to construct his demand schedule.

|  |  |
|---|---|
|  |  |
|  |  |
|  |  |
|  |  |
|  |  |

**b** Show the effect of a price increase from $2.50 to $3.00 on the graph above.

**c** Describe the change illustrated in your graph from question **b**.

_____

_____

_____

ISBN: 9780170241946

**22** Use the following demand curve graph to answer the questions below.

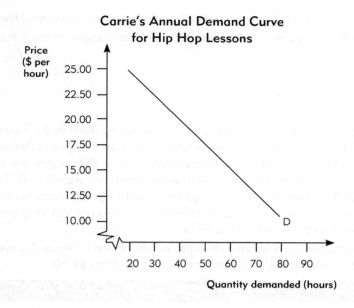

**Carrie's Annual Demand Curve for Hip Hop Lessons**

**a** Use Carrie's demand curve to construct her demand schedule.

| | |
|---|---|
| | |
| | |
| | |
| | |
| | |
| | |
| | |
| | |

**b** Show the effect of a price decrease from $20/hour to $17.50/hour on the graph above.

**23** Use the following demand curve graph to answer the questions below.

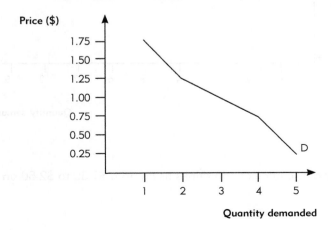

**Rena's Weekly Demand for Peanut Slabs**

ISBN: 9780170241946

a   On the graph above, identify the quantity Rena would demand at the current price of $1.00. Label it Q1.

b   Show the effect of a 25% rise in the price of peanut slabs. Fully label the change.

c   Explain why Rena's quantity demanded of peanut slabs falls as the price rises.

_____

_____

24  Yazmin loves to drink soft drinks. If the tuck shop is selling them at $1.90 each, she will buy five per week. Over the last few weeks, however, the tuck shop has been offering soft drinks at special prices. As a keen Economics student, Yazmin noticed that she bought one more per week when they were $1.70 and another two more each week when they were $1.50. The week that the tuck shop charged $1.30, Yazmin was so excited she bought 10 and made herself ill. She was actually pleased to see the tuck shop increase its prices but this did not last long since as soon as the price rose to $2.50 she could only afford two cans.

a   Use this information to prepare a demand schedule and a demand curve of Yazmin's weekly demand for soft drinks, using the price range of $1.30 to $2.50.

| Yazmin's Weekly Demand for Soft Drinks | |
|---|---|
| | |
| | |
| | |
| | |
| | |
| | |
| | |

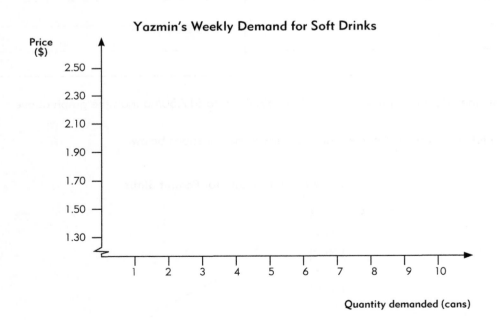

Yazmin's Weekly Demand for Soft Drinks

b   Show the effect of the price of soft drinks rising from $1.30 to $2.50 on your graph.

ISBN: 9780170241946

**c** With reference to your answer to question **b**, fully explain the effect of the price of soft drinks rising from $1.30 to $2.50.

_____

_____

_____

**d** Fully explain a possible flow-on effect that this price change might have on Yazmin.

_____

_____

_____

**25** Bradley has an MP3 player that he was given when he was nine years old. Now that he is 14, he sees that many of his friends have an iPod Touch. Draw a sketch graph of the likely effect that this realisation will have on Bradley's demand for an iPod Touch.

Page 23

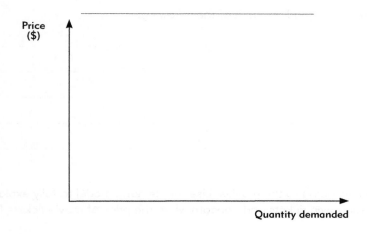

**26** Elena is part of the championship grade netball team for her age. She thinks that an energy drink might give her more stamina for her Saturday game. Use a sketch graph to explain how this will affect her demand for energy drinks.

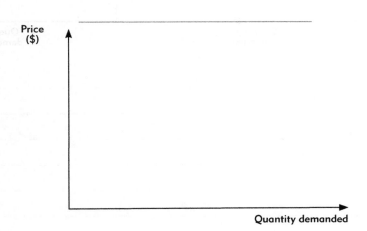

ISBN: 9780170241946

**27** Chelsea and her friends loved a band called Two Ways that was coming to their town to play. It was really difficult to get tickets for their concert. The girls screamed with excitement when they saw the boys in the band. Six months later, the band was no longer popular. Draw a sketch graph to show how this will affect Chelsea's demand for concert tickets for this band.

Page 24

**28** Identify a complementary good for each of the following:

a   DVD _____

b   iPod _____

c   shoes _____

d   Nintendo Wii _____

e   toast _____

**29** Rob and Suzanne love going to the movies. Use the demand model to fully explain what will happen to Rob's demand for movie tickets and popcorn when the price of movie tickets falls.

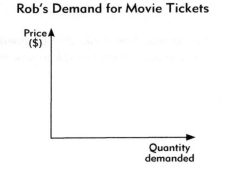

**Rob's Demand for Movie Tickets**

**Rob's Demand for Popcorn**

_____

_____

_____

_____

_____

_____

_____

ISBN: 9780170241946

**1**

**30 a** American hotdogs are part of Peter's weekly meal plan. Describe the relationship between frankfurters and hotdog buns.

_____

_____

**b** Use the demand model to illustrate and fully explain what is likely to happen to Peter's demand for hotdog buns when the price of frankfurters increases.

_____

_____

_____

_____

_____

_____

**31** Explain the difference between a substitute good and a complementary good.

Page 26

_____

_____

_____

_____

**32** Identify a possible substitute good for each of the following.

**a** sandals _____

**b** pineapple juice _____

**c** fish and chips _____

**d** bike _____

**e** Nintendo Wii _____

ISBN: 9780170241946

**33** Jenny has three teenage sons who seem to be constantly hungry and really enjoy eating vegetables. Use the demand model to explain what will happen to Jenny's demand for frozen vegetables when the price of fresh vegetables increases.

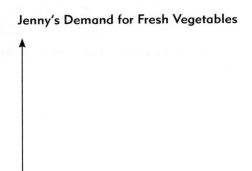

**Jenny's Demand for Fresh Vegetables**

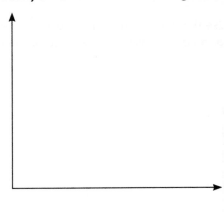

**Jenny's Demand for Frozen Vegetables**

_____

_____

_____

**34** Matt really enjoys getting together a large group of friends to go rock climbing at a local rock climbing centre. Recently, the price of broomball has decreased and Matt and his friends are considering meeting up at the ice skating rink to play broomball instead.

**a** Explain the economic term that best describes the relationship between broomball and rock climbing.

_____

_____

_____

**b** Use the sketch graphs below to explain how the decrease in price in broomball will affect Matt's demand for rock climbing.

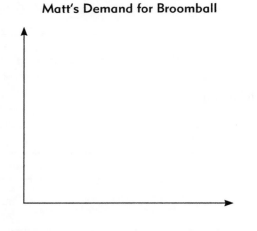

**Matt's Demand for Broomball**          **Matt's Demand for Rock Climbing**

_____

_____

_____

_____

ISBN: 9780170241946

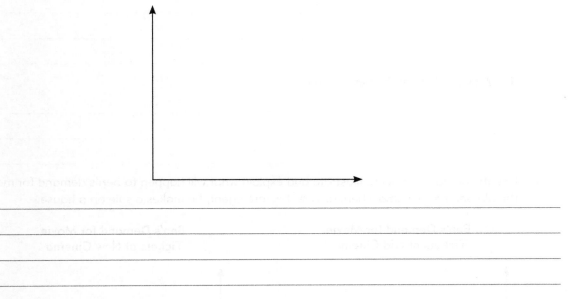

c   Fully explain a flow-on effect this change in demand for broomball might have for Matt.

_____

_____

_____

Page 28

**35** Classify the food below as either a normal good or an inferior good:

- Sausage meat
- Gourmet baked beans
- Homemade baked beans
- Plain biscuits
- Chocolate biscuits
- Eye fillet steak

| Normal good | Inferior good |
|---|---|
|  |  |
|  |  |
|  |  |

**36** Hezekiah usually makes his chilli with lentils as they are reasonably priced. He would prefer to make it with lean mince but it has been too expensive for him. Use the demand model to explain what happens to Hezekiah's demand for lentils when his income increases.

**Hezekiah's Demand for Lentils**

_____

_____

_____

**37** Luka was selected to play in a professional rugby team this season. His income has risen significantly. Use the demand model to show the effect of this on his demand for cereal (a normal good).

**Luka's Demand for Cereal**

ISBN: 9780170241946

**38** Use the demand model to show the effect of a rise in income on the demand for low cost shirts.

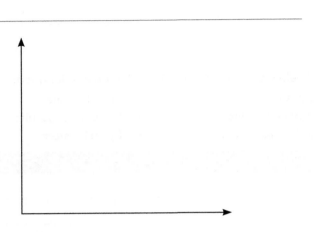

**39** Ben lives near to two movie cinemas. One cinema is old and dated, with old-fashioned, rather uncomfortable chairs but very reasonably priced tickets. The other cinema complex is new, with wide chairs, plenty of leg room and great surround sound, however the tickets are around 25% more expensive.

**a** Identify and explain the type of good, in economic terms, given to each of the movie cinemas.

**i** Movie tickets at the old cinema.

_____

_____

_____

**ii** Movie tickets at the new cinema.

_____

_____

_____

**b** Use the demand model to illustrate and explain what will happen to Ben's demand for movies at the old and new cinema when, as a real estate agent, he makes a sale on a house.

**Ben's Demand for Movie Tickets at Old Cinema**

**Ben's Demand for Movie Tickets at New Cinema**

_____

_____

ISBN: 9780170241946

**40** Match each term from column A with the correct definition in column B in the grid below.

| Column A | Column B | | |
|---|---|---|---|
| 1  complementary goods | a | a change caused by relaxing the condition of ceteris paribus | 1 |
| 2  substitute goods | b | the amount of a good or service that a consumer will be willing and able to buy at various prices | 2 |
| 3  demand | c | goods that are used instead of another good | 3 |
| 4  ceteris paribus | d | a change caused by a decrease in price | 4 |
| 5  movement down the demand curve | e | all other factors remain constant | 5 |
| 6  shift of the demand curve | f | goods that are used together | 6 |

**41** Explain the difference between a normal good and an inferior good.

_____

_____

_____

**42** Complete the Demand for Bananas chart below. The first scenario has been done for you.

| The Demand for Bananas | | | |
|---|---|---|---|
| Scenario | Factor | Graph | Explanation |
| **a**  The price of apples rises | Increase in the price of a substitute good | 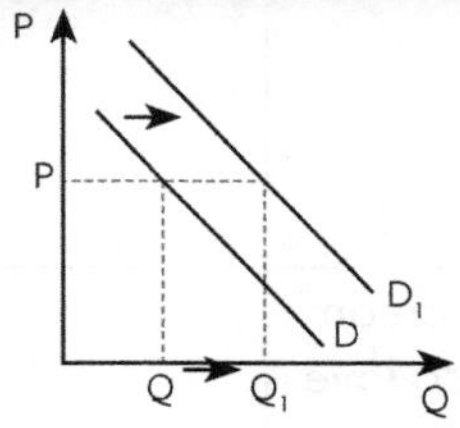 | Apples and bananas are substitute goods. When the price of apples rises, bananas become relatively cheaper, leading to an increase in demand |
| **b**  Income tax rates rise | | 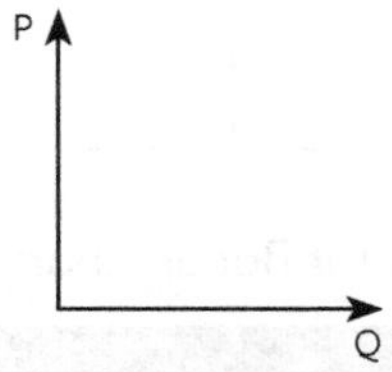 | |
| **c**  Bananas are found to be a great brain food | | 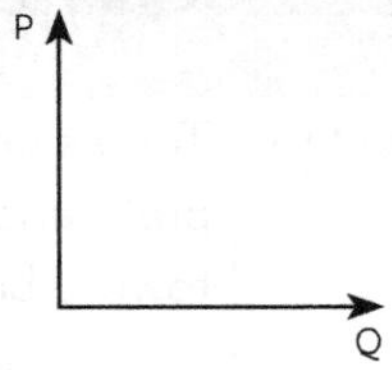 | |
| **d**  The price of bananas rise | | 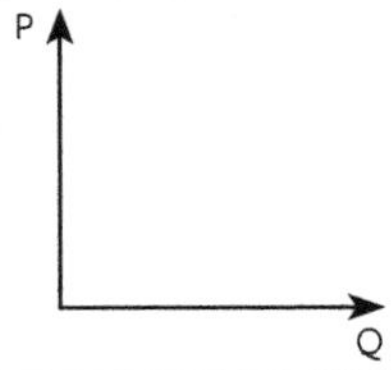 | |

ISBN: 9780170241946

| The Demand for Bananas | | | |
|---|---|---|---|
| Scenario | Factor | Graph | Explanation |
| e | Potassium is found to be causing liver damage. (Bananas are potassium rich) | | 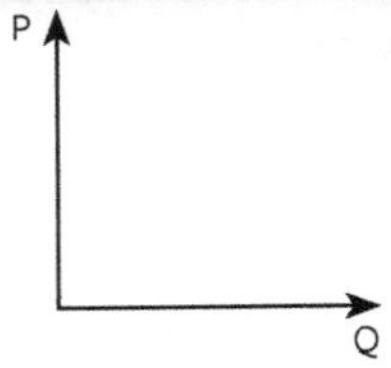 P ↑    → Q | |
| f | The price of oranges decreases | | 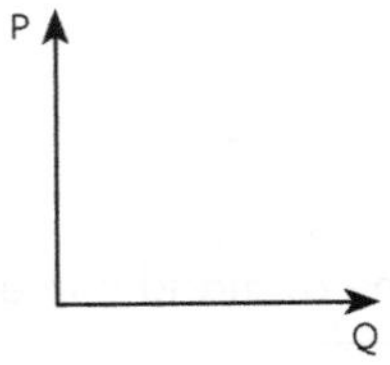 P ↑    → Q | |
| g | Secondary students are to receive government grants to supplement their income | | 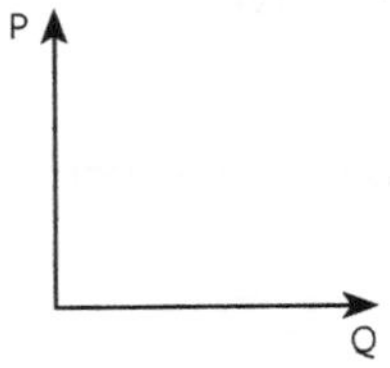 P ↑    → Q | |
| h | The price of pancakes falls (and we love eating bananas with pancakes) | | 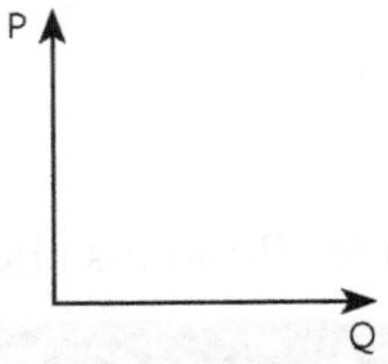 P ↑    → Q | |
| i | The price of bananas falls | | 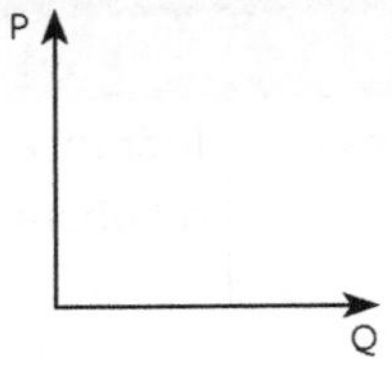 P ↑    → Q | |
| j | The price of ice cream rises (and we also love banana splits) | | 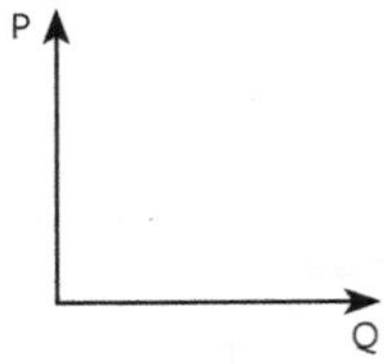 P ↑    → Q | |

43 Complete the Demand for Bacon chart below. The first scenario has been done for you.

| The Demand for Bacon | | | |
|---|---|---|---|
| Scenario | Factor | Graph | Explanation |
| a | Bacon is discovered to be a health food | Tastes and preferences move toward bacon | 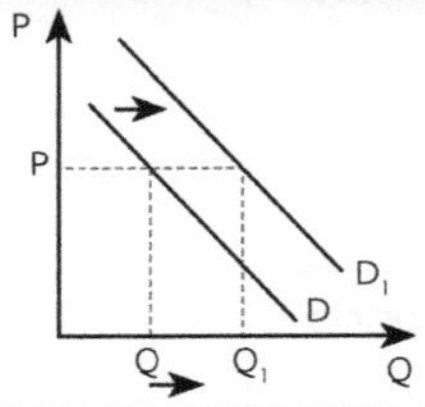 | As bacon becomes more desirable there is an increase in demand and a shift of the curve to the right |
| b | Eggs fall in price | | 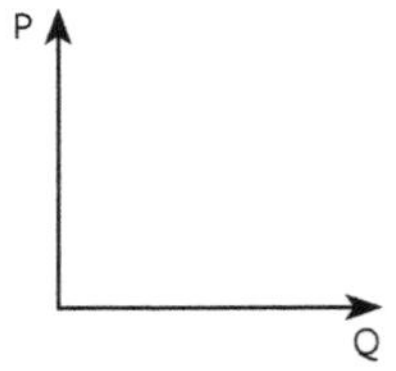 P ↑    → Q | |

ISBN: 9780170241946

## The Demand for Bacon

| | Scenario | Factor | Graph | Explanation |
|---|---|---|---|---|
| c | Price of bacon rises | | 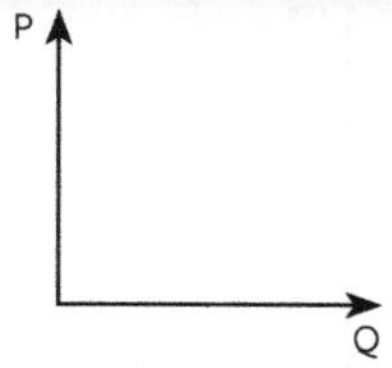 P↑ Q→ | |
| d | New Zealand consumers find bacon too fatty | | 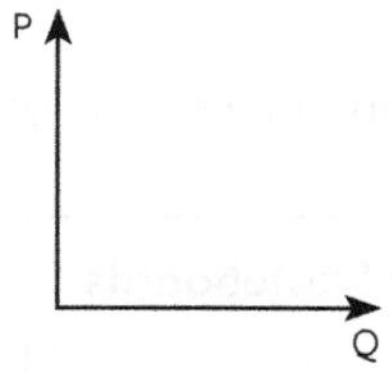 P↑ Q→ | |
| e | | Price of a substitute falls | 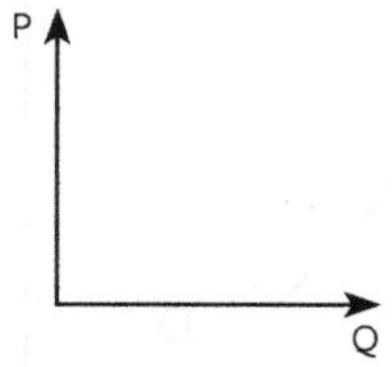 P↑ Q→ | |
| f | | | 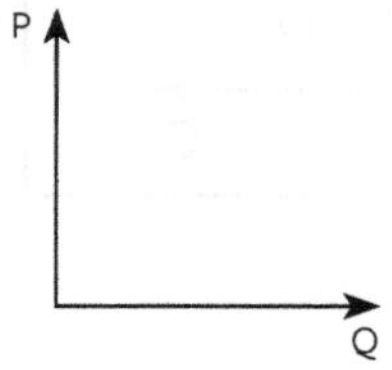 P↑ Q→ | There is an increase in quantity demanded. It is a movement down the demand curve |

**44** Complete the chart below for the Demand for Organic Fruit.

## The Demand for Organic Fruit

| Scenario | Factor | Graph | Explanation |
|---|---|---|---|
| There is a huge advertising campaign for non-organic fruit | | 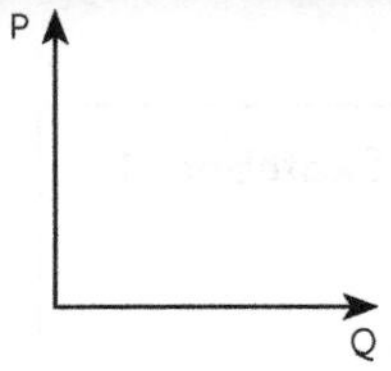 P↑ Q→ | |
| | Price of a substitute _____ | 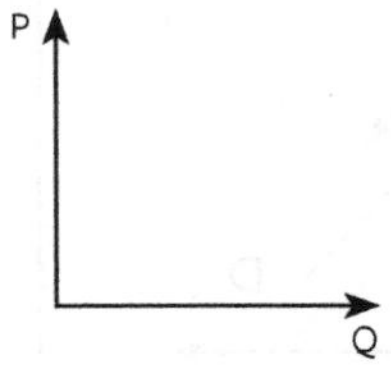 P↑ Q→ | This is an increase in demand. It is a shift to the right of the demand curve |
| New research on the potential negative effects of pesticides is released | | 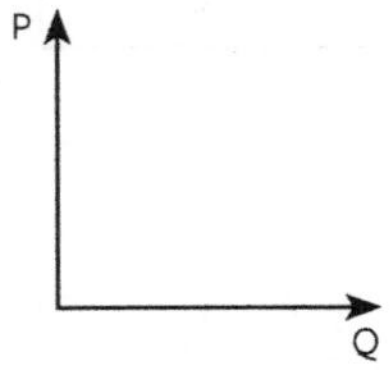 P↑ Q→ | |
| | Disposable income falls | 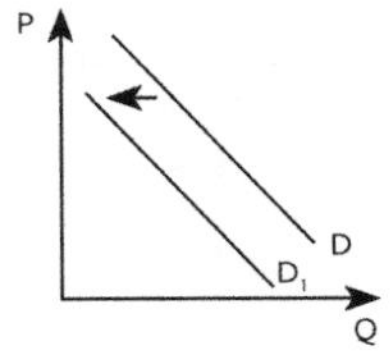 P↑ D D₁ Q→ | |

ISBN: 9780170241946

| The Demand for Organic Fruit | | | |
|---|---|---|---|
| Scenario | Factor | Graph | Explanation |
| Income tax rates fall | | 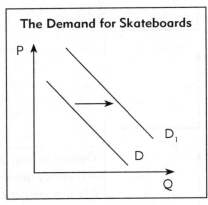 P Q | |

**45** Complete each graph and identify all of the possible reasons for each of the changes shown on the graphs.

**a**

The Demand for Skateboards

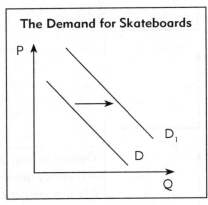

_____

_____

_____

_____

**b**

The Demand for Skateboards

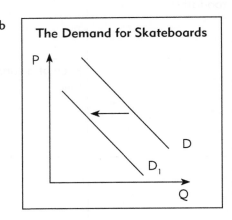

_____

_____

_____

_____

**c**

The Demand for Skateboards

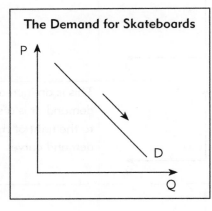

_____

_____

_____

_____

**d**

The Demand for Skateboards

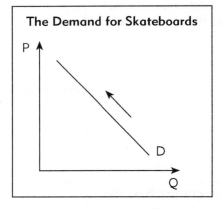

_____

_____

_____

_____

ISBN: 9780170241946

**e**

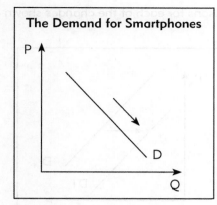

The Demand for Smartphones

_____
_____
_____
_____

**f**

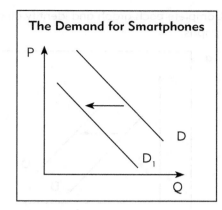

The Demand for Smartphones

_____
_____
_____
_____

**g**

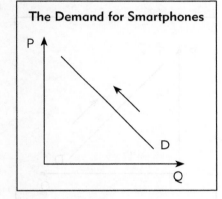

The Demand for Smartphones

_____
_____
_____
_____
_____

**h**

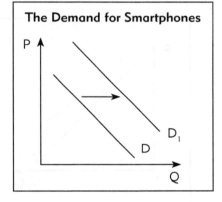

The Demand for Smartphones

_____
_____
_____
_____
_____

ISBN: 9780170241946

**46** Complete each graph and identify all of the possible reasons for each of the changes shown on the graphs.

a

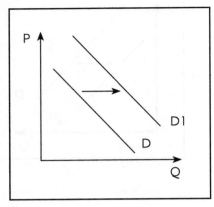

_____
_____
_____
_____
_____

b

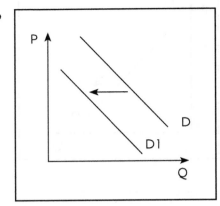

_____
_____
_____
_____
_____

c

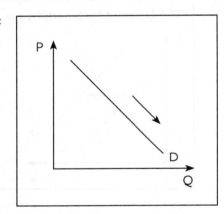

_____
_____
_____
_____
_____

d

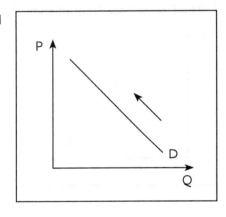

_____
_____
_____
_____
_____

Page 37

**47** The table below shows the percentage of New Zealand household expenditure in 1980 and in 2008. Use the table to answer the questions that follow.

| Group | 1980 | 2008 |
|---|---|---|
| | Percent | |
| Food | 19.70 | 17.83 |
| Alcoholic beverages and tobacco | 9.13 | 6.76 |
| Clothing and footwear | 7.30 | 4.48 |
| Housing and household utilities | 16.63 | 22.75 |
| Household contents and services | 9.17 | 5.26 |

ISBN: 9780170241946

| Group | 1980 | 2008 |
|---|---|---|
| | Percent | |
| Health | 1.46 | 5.09 |
| Transport | 16.93 | 16.18 |
| Communication | 1.46 | 3.21 |
| Recreation and culture | 8.04 | 9.54 |
| Education | 0.36 | 1.78 |
| Miscellaneous goods and services | 9.80 | 7.12 |
| All groups | 100.00 | 100.00 |

(Source: www.stats.govt.nz)

a   Classify each item on the table as either a necessity, basic want or luxury.

| Necessity | Basic want | Luxury |
|---|---|---|
| | | |
| | | |
| | | |
| | | |
| | | |

b   Identify three significant changes between 1980 and 2008. For each change identified, give a possible reason for the change.

i   _____

_____

_____

_____

_____

ii   _____

_____

_____

_____

_____

iii   _____

_____

_____

_____

_____

c   If an average household's disposable income in 2008 was $1234, use the table above to calculate the amount a typical household would spend on:

i   food _____

ii   housing _____

**1**

  **iii** transport _____

  **iv** clothing and footwear _____

**d** Andrew has not studied Economics before. He looked at the table above and concluded that 'households spent less on food in 2008 than they did in 1980.' Explain to Andrew why this is probably not true.

_____

_____

_____

_____

_____

**e** Prepare two pie graphs to show the percentage of household expenditure in 1980 and 2008.

**48** Write a 'breaking news' article explaining the relationship between household income and consumption patterns. Record it as a podcast, if possible.

_____

_____

_____

_____

_____

_____

_____

_____

_____

ISBN: 9780170241946

# Producer decisions about production

1 Define the following terms:

Page 39

a good _____

_____

b service _____

_____

c firm _____

_____

d industry _____

_____

e interdependence _____

_____

2 William works for an engineering firm. Explain how William relies on the producer sector and how the producer sector relies on William as part of the household sector.

_____

_____

_____

_____

_____

_____

3 a List five private sector businesses that are likely to be in business to make a profit.

b List five voluntary organisations.

Page 40

_____    _____

_____    _____

_____    _____

_____    _____

_____    _____

**Page 41**

4   Distinguish between private and public sector producers.

_____

_____

_____

5   Use your research skills to identify the names of six State Owned Enterprises.

_____

_____

_____

_____

_____

_____

6   Name two government departments (or ministries).

_____

_____

7   Explain the difference between the purpose or main goal of a government department and the purpose or main goal of a State Owned Enterprise.

_____

_____

_____

_____

**Page 44**

8   Match each term in column A with the correct definition in column B in the grid below.

| Column A | | Column B |
| --- | --- | --- |
| 1 intermediate good | a | A single business or producer |
| 2 service | b | Goods the government or society consider beneficial for you |
| 3 profit | c | Goods are provided by the government out of taxation |
| 4 merit good | d | A group of businesses that produce a similar good or service |
| 5 central government | e | A human-made good used in the production of other goods and services |
| 6 collective good | f | The reward to business owners, the difference between revenue earned and expenses paid |
| 7 capital good | g | A finished good which is of little use until it is used in the production of another good |
| 8 firm | h | When something is done for you |
| 9 industry | i | Elected representatives who make decisions for the country as a whole |

| | |
| --- | --- |
| 1 | |
| 2 | |
| 3 | |
| 4 | |
| 5 | |
| 6 | |
| 7 | |
| 8 | |
| 9 | |

ISBN: 9780170241946

**9** Describe what is meant by the term **profit maximisation**.

_____

_____

**10** Explain why market share is not a key goal of the Ministry of Education.

_____

_____

_____

**11** Distinguish between a capital good and a consumer good.

Page 45

_____

_____

**12** Explain how a cellphone can be both a capital good and a consumer good.

_____

_____

_____

_____

**13** Identify four commercial and three non-commercial goals that business owners or managers might have for their business.

**Commercial goals** _____

_____

_____

_____

**Non-commercial goals** _____

_____

_____

_____

**14** Explain the difference between a firm and an industry, and provide an example of each.

_____

_____

_____

_____

**15** Identify five key service industries that businesses rely on.

_____

_____

_____

ISBN: 9780170241946

**16** Explain how these key service industries and other businesses are interdependent.

_____

_____

_____

_____

_____

**17** Identify three functions that a marketing firm might carry out.

_____

_____

_____

**18** Use a sheet of paper to create a mind map encompassing the content of this unit so far.

Page 47 (top) **19** Explain the difference between labour and entrepreneurship.

_____

_____

**20** Identify the payment that labour earns.

_____

**21** Identify the payment that entrepreneurs earn.

_____

**22** Yvonne has recently inherited $100 000. She will either buy a rental property with it, or start a business. Fully explain two possible consequences for _each_ option.

**Rental property** _____

_____

_____

_____

**Start a business** _____

_____

_____

_____

**23** Describe the qualities of an entrepreneur.

_____

_____

ISBN: 9780170241946

**24** Define the following terms:

a investment _____

_____

b intermediate goods _____

_____

c capital goods _____

_____

d interest rates _____

_____

**25** Describe four capital goods that a supermarket would use.

_____
_____
_____
_____

**26** Explain the relationship between investment and interest rates.

_____
_____
_____
_____

**27** Describe one example of investment that a producer might undertake for their orchard.

_____
_____

**28** Josh, owner of *Electrics on Call*, has the option of borrowing in order to buy a new van for his firm. Outline possible consequences for Josh if he chooses to do this.

_____
_____
_____
_____
_____

**29** Use an example to explain the difference between renewable and non-renewable resources.

**Page 49**

_____
_____
_____

**30** Identify one renewable resource that might be used by *Stenner Architects Limited*.

_____

**31** Identify one non-renewable resource that *Stenner Architects Limited* might use.

_____

**32** Distinguish between the terms recycle and reuse.

_____

_____

_____

_____

**33** *Stenner Architects Limited* decide to purchase a fleet of electric cars instead of petrol powered cars. Fully explain possible consequences of this choice on the firm and on society.

_____

_____

_____

_____

_____

_____

_____

_____

_____

**34** 'Ecological sustainability' is a key value identified in the New Zealand Curriculum. Explain what is meant by this term.

_____

_____

_____

_____

_____

_____

Page 51 (top)

> 'Whatungarongaro te tangata toitū te whenua ...
> People pass on but the land remains' (Maori proverb)

**35** Explain how this proverb relates to the significance of sustainability for Maori.

_____

_____

_____

_____

32

ISBN: 9780170241946

**36** Use your research skills to describe what is means by the term rahui. Explain how a rahui will affect the use of kaimoana (seafood).

_____

_____

_____

_____

_____

_____

_____

_____

**37** Classify the following terms as either a natural resource, a human-made resource, or a human resource in the table below.

Page 51–52

- climate
- nurse
- natural gas
- train tracks
- crude oil
- iron sands
- hammer
- stethoscope

- solar energy
- pilot
- waiter
- geothermal energy
- doctor
- menu
- welder
- truck

- plumber
- dairy owner
- deep sea fish
- Pacific Rose apple
- airport
- accountant

| Natural resource | Human-made resource | Human resource |
|---|---|---|
|  |  |  |
|  |  |  |
|  |  |  |
|  |  |  |
|  |  |  |
|  |  |  |
|  |  |  |
|  |  |  |
|  |  |  |
|  |  |  |

**38** For each of the natural resources you have identified above, use highlighters and a key to classify them as either renewable or non-renewable.

| Key | Renewable | Non-renewable |
|---|---|---|

**39** Todd is an orchardist in Kerikeri. Explain why oranges are not a resource for Todd's business.

_____

_____

_____

ISBN: 9780170241946

**40** Use the following diagram structure to identify 10 resources and any potential outputs for each of the following production processes. The first example has been done for you.

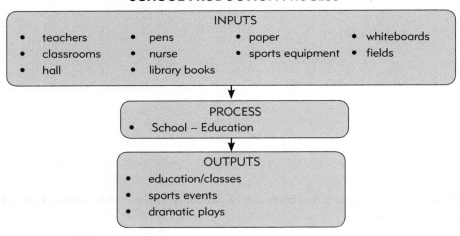

**SCHOOL PRODUCTION PROCESS**

**INPUTS**
- teachers
- classrooms
- hall
- pens
- nurse
- library books
- paper
- sports equipment
- whiteboards
- fields

**PROCESS**
- School – Education

**OUTPUTS**
- education/classes
- sports events
- dramatic plays

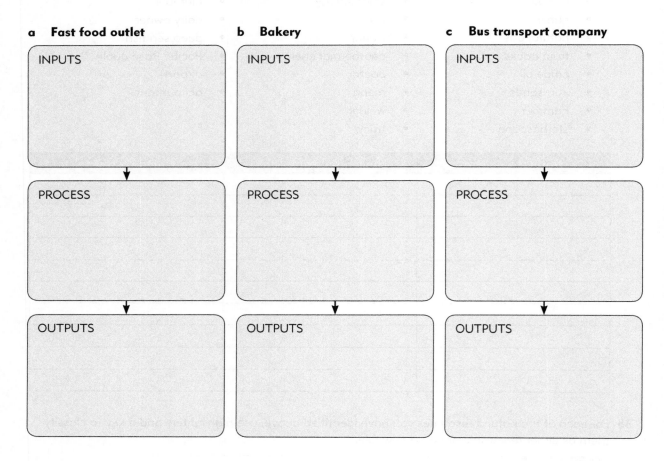

**a  Fast food outlet**

INPUTS

PROCESS

OUTPUTS

**b  Bakery**

INPUTS

PROCESS

OUTPUTS

**c  Bus transport company**

INPUTS

PROCESS

OUTPUTS

**41** Suggest at least one consequence if producers do not choose to support sustainable use of resources.

_____

_____

ISBN: 9780170241946

42 Calculate productivity per worker in the following cases:

| | Total production | Number of workers | Productivity per worker |
|---|---|---|---|
| a | 1500 pizzas per week | 12 | |
| b | 156 corkboards per week | 3 | |
| c | 36 building plans per year | 2 | |
| d | 56 coffees per hour | 2 | |

43 Jacob and Bella own a small garage where they specialise in repairing and restoring old motorbikes. As demand for their services increased, they employed Edward to help with the restorations. Over time they also employed Sam, Jared and Paul. The following table outlines the productivity of the business as Jacob and Bella employed more staff:

a Complete the table by adding the missing data.

| Labour Productivity for Bikes Repaired, per Month | | | |
|---|---|---|---|
| Month | Number of staff | Bikes repaired | Bikes repaired per worker |
| 1 | 2 | 10 | |
| 2 | 3 | | 6 |
| 3 | 4 | 28 | |
| 4 | | 35 | 7 |
| 5 | 6 | | 6.5 |

b Distinguish between production and productivity.

_____

_____

_____

_____

c Explain possible positive consequence of an increase in productivity for Bella and Jacob's business.

_____

_____

_____

Page 55
(bottom)

44 Identify three industries that are likely to be labour intensive.

_____

_____

_____

45 Identify three industries that are likely to be capital intensive.

_____

_____

_____

**46** Explain two advantages of capital intensive production over labour intensive production.

_____

_____

_____

_____

**47** _Fehi's Packaging_ are changing their production process towards more capital intensive methods. Explain both potential positive and negative consequences of this change for their workers.

**Positive consequences** _____

_____

_____

**Negative consequences** _____

_____

_____

**48** Tim owns a large business that specialises in the production of soft drink. Five years ago there were 35 workers on a production line in the factory. Now there are 15 employees who operate automated machines 24 hours a day. Explain whether the production process of the soft drink has become more capital or more labour intensive.

_____

_____

_____

_____

_____

_____

Page 57

**49** Define the term technology.

_____

**50** Chris owns a lawnmowing and landscaping business. Explain how new technology could lead to increased productivity in his firm.

_____

_____

_____

**51** A firm that Riley works for has informed him that new technology is now able to perform the tasks that Riley normally carries out. Explain a positive consequence for the firm if they introduce this new technology. Explain one possible consequence for Riley.

**Positive consequence for the firm** _____

_____

**Possible consequence for Riley** _____

_____

ISBN: 9780170241946

**52** Define the term investment.

_____

**53** Explain the link between investment and interest rates.

_____

_____

_____

**54** The Reserve Bank of New Zealand (RBNZ) has a huge influence on interest rates in New Zealand. Use your research skills to answer the following questions:

  **a** Describe the main roles of the Reserve Bank of New Zealand.

_____

_____

_____

  **b** Identify the current Governor of the RBNZ.

_____

  **c** Identify what OCR stands for. _____

  **d** Briefly explain what the OCR is. _____

_____

_____

  **e** Briefly explain how an increase in the OCR might have an effect on a business that wished to increase investment.

_____

_____

_____

**55** Explain how increased investment might impact on productivity.

_____

_____

_____

_____

**56** Define division of labour.

Page 60

_____

_____

_____

ISBN: 9780170241946

**57** Read the case study below and answer the questions that follow:

### Division of labour in pin production

Who would have thought there was so much to manufacturing a pin? In his book *Wealth of Nations* (1776), Adam Smith described how the division of labour could be applied to the making of a pin:

'One man draws out the wire, another straights it, a third cuts it, a fourth points it, a fifth grinds it at the top for receiving the head; to make the head required two or three distinct operations; to put it on, is a peculiar business, to whiten the pins is another; it is even a trade by itself to put them into the paper; and the important business of making a pin is, in this manner, divided into about eighteen distinct operations, which, in some manufactories, are all performed by distinct hands, though in others the same man will sometimes perform two or three of them.'

Smith points out that by applying the division of labour principles to the pin factory there is an increase in productivity of somewhere between 240 and 4800 times!

a   Assume there were 10 people working in the pin factory. Calculate productivity per worker per day, if they produced 20 pins in one day.

_____

b   After the implementation of the division of labour, output increased to 48 000 pins per day for the 10 workers. Calculate the new productivity per worker per day.

_____

c   Use the formula below to calculate the percentage increase in productivity with the new production method in place.

**Percentage increase**

$$\frac{(\text{New figure} - \text{old figure})}{\text{Old figure}} \times \frac{100}{1}$$

_____

d   Imagine it is 1776 and you are a worker in the pin factory. It is your job to put the pin into the paper. Write a letter to your parents, who live in another country, describing your job and how you feel about it.

_____

_____

_____

_____

_____

_____

_____

_____

_____

_____

_____

_____

ISBN: 9780170241946

_____

**58** Sharda owns a hair salon in Christchurch. Her business is going well, but her goal is to improve her market share. She has come to you for some advice.

Page 61

**a** Her first question is about investment. She has heard people say that she could increase investment. She thinks that means putting her savings into the bank. Explain to Sharda what investment means, in Economic terms.

_____

_____

**b** Another term Sharda has heard is division of labour. Explain to Sharda what this term means and how it could be useful in her business.

_____

_____

**c** Explain to Sharda each of the ways that she could improve productivity in her firm.

_____

_____

_____

_____

_____

**d** It was recently announced by the RBNZ that the Official Cash Rate would rise, leading to an increase in interest rates. Explain to Sharda how this might affect her choices regarding investment and technology. Be specific and use data to assist your explanation.

_____

_____

_____

_____

_____

_____

_____

ISBN: 9780170241946

e  Identify possible consequences of improving the productivity in this business:

   i   For the business.

_____

_____

_____

   ii   For the customers.

_____

_____

_____

**59** Explain the links between improved labour productivity and profit.

_____

_____

_____

**Page 63**

**60** Define productivity.

_____

**61** Distinguish between internal and external factors affecting productivity.

_____

_____

_____

_____

_____

**62** Complete the following table.

| Increased productivity | |
|---|---|
| Advantages | Disadvantages |
| | |
| | |

ISBN: 9780170241946

|  |  |
|  |  |

**63** Outline the possible consequences on the workers if there is an increase in productivity.

_____

_____

_____

_____

**64** Use a blank sheet of paper to draw a mind map to summarise productivity choices of producers.

**65** Leah and Seth own a bakery where they make everything they sell. At the beginning of the year they were making 500 units per day (including everything from doughnuts to sausage rolls). The total cost of this daily production was $1000. Over the next two years they increased the scale of their operations. They invested in new equipment, hired more staff and extended their premises. By this time production had increased to 3200 units per day at a total cost of $5500 per day.

Page 64

**a** Distinguish between average cost and total cost.

_____

_____

**b** Calculate the bakery's average cost for both periods (at the beginning of year 1 and the end of year 2).

_____

_____

**c** Calculate the percentage change in average cost between the two periods of time.

_____

_____

**d** Suggest one possible reason for the change in average cost.

_____

_____

**66** Define the term economies of scale, and explain it in simple terms for someone who has not studied Economics before.

_____

_____

_____

_____

ISBN: 9780170241946

**67** A friend of yours was away from school yesterday when you learned about the various reasons for economies of scale. Write a script of how you will explain to her what she missed.

_____

_____

_____

_____

_____

_____

_____

_____

_____

_____

Page 67

**68** Match the term in column A with the correct definition in column B using the grid below.

| Column A | | Column B |
|---|---|---|
| 1 economies of scale | a | cost per unit |
| 2 average cost | b | as the scale of operations increases, average costs of production fall |
| 3 technical economies | c | specialisation of management as a result of increased size of the firm, and resulting in decreasing average costs |
| 4 total cost | d | economies of scale resulting from promotional expenses being spread across greater output, bulk buying benefits and best buys because of specialised buyers |
| 5 managerial economies | e | the sum of all of the costs involved in getting goods or services ready for sale |
| 6 diseconomies of scale | f | as the scale of operations increases, average costs of production rise |
| 7 marketing economies | g | benefits gained in terms of borrowing due to the larger scale of production |
| 8 division of labour | h | when a production process is split into many parts, each carried out by a different worker or group of workers |
| 9 financial economies | i | lower average costs because of the use of machinery and production processes that large firms can benefit from |

| | |
|---|---|
| 1 | |
| 2 | |
| 3 | |
| 4 | |
| 5 | |
| 6 | |
| 7 | |
| 8 | |
| 9 | |

**69** Explain the link between economies of scale and productivity.

_____

_____

**70** Fully explain how greater economies of scale could affect the profits of a firm.

_____

_____

_____

ISBN: 9780170241946

**71** Chris and Lucy worked for a large educational department which had become larger by joining several smaller departments together. However, it became so large that management did not know their staff and communication became impersonal. The management were so overwhelmed by the enormity of the job that they were cranky with the staff, and many contracts were not ready for staff before they started teaching, their offices were not ready and they did not have internet access when they should have. Staff felt unvalued and discouraged, productivity started to fall and some staff even left the faculty.

**a** Explain how the department might have thought it could benefit from being larger.

_____

_____

_____

_____

_____

_____

_____

_____

**b** Identify and explain the term used to describe the situation when the department became too large.

_____

_____

**72** Use a blank sheet of paper to draw a mind map on economies and diseconomies of scale.

**73** Suggest a good or a service that the following producers could potentially diversify into:

Page 64

| Current business | A business it could diversify into |
|---|---|
| **a** Pratima's Publishing | |
| **b** The $3 Shop | |
| **c** Dorothy's Second Hand Bookshop | |
| **d** Homeopathy with Rose | |

**Page 69
(bottom)**

**74** Complete the following chart.

| Diversification | |
|---|---|
| **Advantages** | **Disadvantages** |
|  |  |
|  |  |
|  |  |

**75** Use the phrase *'don't put all of your eggs in one basket'* to explain the main benefit of expanding through diversification.

_____

_____

_____

_____

_____

_____

**Page 71–73**

**76** Match the term in column A with the correct definition in column B in the grid below.

| Column A | | Column B |
|---|---|---|
| **1** diversification | **a** | merging with or taking over a related business that is at the same stage of the production process |
| **2** merge | **b** | starting, taking over or merging with a firm which is in a different type of business to the original business |
| **3** takeover | **c** | when a dominant firm buys a share in another firm |
| **4** vertical integration | **d** | taking over or merging with a firm which is in a related area of business but is at a different stage of the production process |
| **5** horizontal integration | **e** | joining together with another firm for mutual benefit |

| | |
|---|---|
| 1 | |
| 2 | |
| 3 | |
| 4 | |
| 5 | |

ISBN: 9780170241946

**77** Fully explain how business expansion is likely to affect:

   **i**   productivity of labour _____

_____

_____

_____

_____

   **ii**  profits of the firm _____

_____

_____

_____

_____

**78** Maree and Nick Plummer own a small clothing firm called *Plummer Enterprises*. They recently decided to expand their business by moving into the market for gourmet cookware.

   **a**  Identify the name of this type of business expansion.

_____

   **b**  Explain one reason why Plummer Enterprises might expand in this way.

_____

_____

Maree and Nick have an opportunity to merge with another clothing firm.

   **c**  Identify the name of this type of business expansion. Be specific.

_____

   **d**  Explain two advantages that Maree and Nick could experience as a result of the merger you identified in question c.

      **i**  _____

_____

      **ii**  _____

_____

**79** Identify the type of business expansion each of the following case studies illustrates:

| | Column B | Business expansion |
|---|---|---|
| **a** | Harry owns *Exquisite Espresso*, where they roast, pack and sell coffee. He plans to buy the business of a coffee bean grower. | |
| **b** | Cleo the clown has an entertainment business where she is hired out to entertain at children's parties. She has recently decided to expand her business into party planning. | |
| **c** | Stuart is a dairy farmer who is going to merge with a neighbouring dairy farm. | |
| **d** | Stuart the dairy farmer is now starting a gift basket business. | |
| **e** | Flora grows flowers and sells them to florists. She has decided to buy her own florist shop. | |

**80** Darren is a panelbeater who has the opportunity to take over another panelbeating business.

   **a** Name this type of business expansion.

_____

   **b** Identify one consequence of this decision for each of the following:

| Affected person or group | Consequence of this business expansion decision |
|---|---|
| **a** Darren | |
| **b** Workers at Darren's firm | |
| **c** Workers at the new firm | |
| **d** Customers | |

**81** Complete the following fishbone diagram to summarise the key points of this chapter.

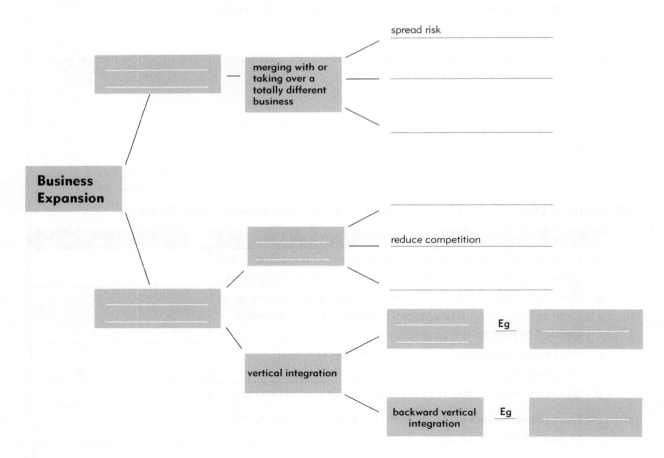

ISBN: 9780170241946

Page 74

82 Using your local newspaper collect a range of different examples of firms using price competition to sell their products. Find at least one example for each price strategy (discounts, sales, 'two for one' or 'buy one get one free' deals, or permanent lower price policies such as 'We won't be beaten on price'.

Page 77

83 For each of the following categories of product differentiation, find an example from your own experience (or the experience of someone in your household), where this has influenced you to purchase a product.

| Product differentiation | Personal example |
| --- | --- |
| Location | |
| Branding | |
| Sponsorship | |
| Loyalty schemes | |
| Packaging | |
| Advertising | |
| Service | |
| Competitions | |
| Gift with purchase | |

Page 80

84 Explain why price wars only occur in markets with a few sellers.

_____

_____

_____

**85** Identify five markets or products that have only a few sellers.

_____

**86** Sort the following into either price or non-price competition in the table below.

| Price competition | Non-price competition |
|---|---|
|  |  |
|  |  |
|  |  |
|  |  |
|  |  |

**87** Explain the difference between product variation and product differentiation.

_____
_____
_____
_____

ISBN: 9780170241946

88 Use different coloured highlighters to classify each example of non-price competition in question 86 as either product variation or product differentiation. Complete the key below.

| Key | Product variation | Product differentiation |
|---|---|---|

89 Provide four examples of generic products or services that are referred to by a brand name. Clingfilm, for example, is commonly referred to as Gladwrap.

| Product | Brand name it is referred to as |
|---|---|
| Clingfilm | Gladwrap |
|  |  |
|  |  |
|  |  |
|  |  |

90 Describe your favourite television advertisement. Analyse how effective it is in terms of influencing you to buy the good or service.

_____

_____

_____

_____

_____

91 A friend of yours is a plumber. She sends you an email asking for advice because she is struggling to get customers due to the number of other plumbers in her area. Compose an email in reply, giving your friend comprehensive advice on how she might compete in this market. Be specific and ensure you fully explain the advantages and disadvantages of each option.

_____

_____

_____

_____

_____

_____

_____

_____

_____

_____

_____

_____

_____

92 Use a blank sheet of paper to create a mind map to summarise the information on price and non-price competition.

# 3 Producer choices using supply

Page 84

**1** Define supply. _____

_____

**2** State the Law of Supply. _____

_____

**3** Imagine you make picture frames decorated with sea shells and glitter. Explain why you would make more frames available at higher prices than lower prices.

_____

_____

Page 86

**4** Use the following supply schedule to construct a supply curve below.

| Plumbers R Us Limited Weekly Supply Schedule of Pipes | |
|---|---|
| Price ($ per metre) | Quantity supplied |
| 10 | 300 |
| 12 | 400 |
| 14 | 500 |
| 16 | 600 |
| 18 | 700 |
| 20 | 800 |
| 22 | 900 |
| 24 | 1000 |

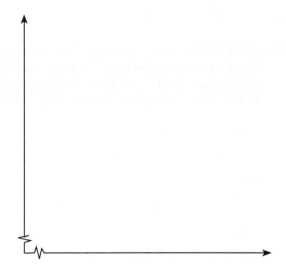

**5** Use the following supply curve to derive a supply schedule.

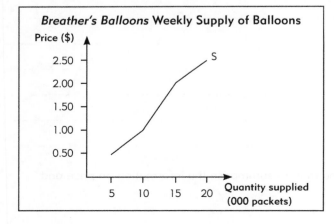

| | |
|---|---|
| | |
| | |
| | |
| | |
| | |
| | |

50

ISBN: 9780170241946

**6** Use the following supply schedule to construct a supply curve and answer the questions that follow.

| Rewi Ramikin's Weekly Supply of Macaroni Cheese | |
|---|---|
| Price ($) | Quantity (000 bowls) |
| 20 | 4 |
| 15 | 3 |
| 10 | 2 |
| 5 | 1 |

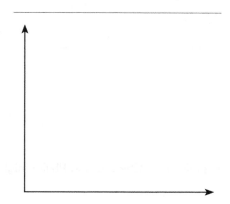

**a** Show the effect of a price rise from $10 to $15. Fully label your graph.

**b** Calculate the change in quantity supplied.

**c** Show the effect of a price fall from $20 to $5. Fully label your graph.

**d** Calculate the change in quantity supplied.

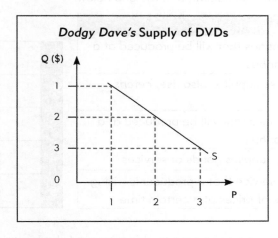

Dodgy Dave's Supply of DVDs

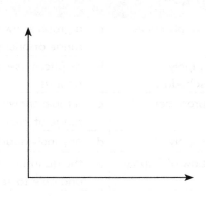

**7** The graph for Dodgy Dave's supply of DVDs drawn above is incorrect. Re-draw the graph correctly.

**8** Phillip and Chelsea sell olive oil at the Nelson markets. The weekly supply schedule for their firm is shown below.

| P&C Oil's Weekly Supply Schedule of Olive Oil | |
|---|---|
| Price ($) | Quantity supplied (bottles) |
| 4.00 | 50 |
| 5.00 | 60 |
| 6.00 | 80 |
| 7.00 | 110 |

**a** Draw and fully label P&C Oil's weekly supply curve of olive oil.

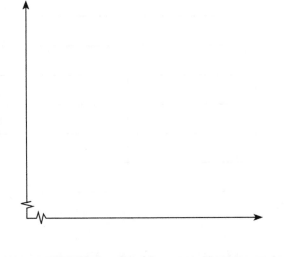

**b** Show the effect of a price decrease from $7.00 to $6.00.

ISBN: 9780170241946

**c** Use the Law of Supply to fully explain what happened in question **b** above.

_____

_____

_____

_____

_____

**d** Explain what Chelsea and Phillip might decide to do if the price of olive oil fell below $2.00.

_____

_____

_____

_____

_____

Page 88

**9** Match the terms in column A with the correct definition in column B in the grid below.

| Column A | | Column B |
|---|---|---|
| 1 supply curve | a | a graph showing the quantities that will be produced at a range of prices, *ceteris paribus* |
| 2 supply schedule | b | as prices rise, the quantities supplied also rise, *ceteris paribus* |
| 3 producer | c | a table showing the quantities that will be produced at a range of prices, *ceteris paribus* |
| 4 supply | d | any individual or firm that supplies goods or services |
| 5 Law of Supply | e | the quantity of a good or service that a producer is willing and able to sell at a range of prices at a certain time |

| | |
|---|---|
| 1 | |
| 2 | |
| 3 | |
| 4 | |
| 5 | |

**10** Pam owns and operates a business called *Soul Care*, where she goes to elderly people's homes to give pedicures and take care of their feet and toenails. The price she can charge per visit is the most important factor in determining how many hours each day she will work. At $8 per visit she would be willing to see three clients a day. At $12 per visit, she would be willing to see six clients per day. At $16 she would visit nine clients, and at $20 she would be prepared to visit 12 clients.

**a** Complete Pam's supply schedule for pedicures per day.

**b** Draw a fully labelled graph to show *Soul Care*'s supply per day.

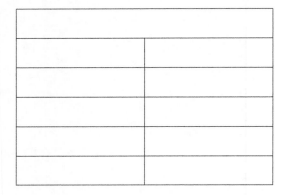

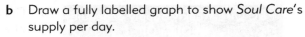

ISBN: 9780170241946

c Fully explain what Pam is likely to do if the price of a pedicure was increased to $28.

_____
_____
_____
_____
_____

11 Use the supply model to explain the difference between the way a producer will react to a change in price compared to a change in costs.

Page 94–96

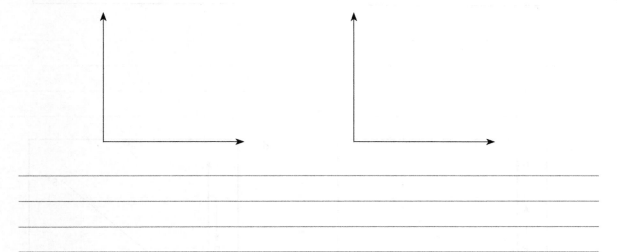

_____
_____
_____
_____

12 Complete the links in this table, using different coloured pens for each change. One set of links has been completed as an example.

| Change | Results in | Shown as | Graph |
|---|---|---|---|
| Increase in price | Increase in supply | Movement down | |
| Increase in costs | Decrease in quantity supplied | Shift right | |
| Improved technology | Increase in quantity supplied | Shift left | |
| Decrease in price | Decrease in supply | Movement up | |

ISBN: 9780170241946

**13** Give possible reasons for each of the change shown on the graphs below.

a

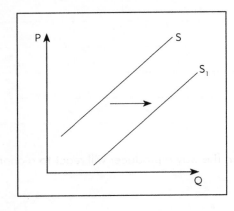

b

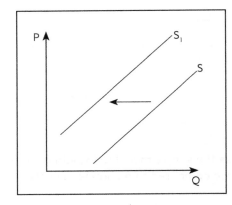

_____

_____

_____

_____

c

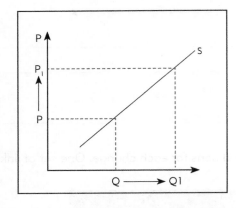

d

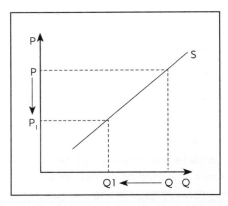

_____

_____

_____

_____

**14** Complete the table below. The first scenario has been done for you as an example.

| The Supply of Josie's Amazing Hot Sausages in Bread | | | |
| --- | --- | --- | --- |
| Scenario | Factor | Graph | Explanation |
| Workers wages rise | Increase in costs of production | P, S₁, S graph | The increase in costs makes the business less profitable and so Josie will supply less at each price. There is a _decrease in supply_. |
| Bread falls in price | | P, Q graph | |

ISBN: 9780170241946

## The Supply of Josie's Amazing Hot Sausages in Bread

| Scenario | Factor | Graph | Explanation |
|---|---|---|---|
| | Improved technology | P, Q | |
| | | P, Q | This is an increase in *quantity supplied*. It is a *movement* up the supply curve. |
| | Costs of production fall | P, Q | There is an increase in *supply* as it has become more profitable. It is a *shift to the right* of the supply curve. |
| Hamburgers rise in price | | P, Q | |
| | Price of other goods we make falls | P, Q | |

15 Finn's movie theatre can use its machine to make popcorn or caramel corn.

   a  Use the supply model to fully explain what would happen to the supply of popcorn if the price of caramel corn increased.

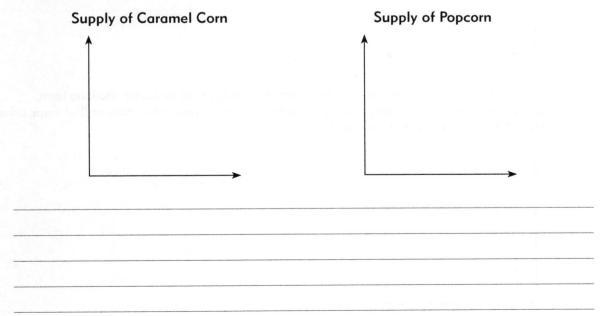

**Supply of Caramel Corn**          **Supply of Popcorn**

_____

_____

_____

_____

_____

ISBN: 9780170241946

**b** Use the supply model to fully explain what would happen to the supply of popcorn if the price of caramel corn decreased.

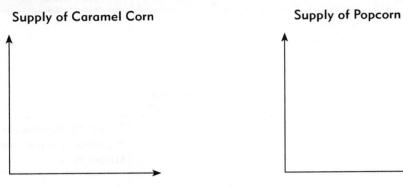

Supply of Caramel Corn          Supply of Popcorn

_____

_____

_____

_____

_____

_____

_____

_____

Page 98

**16** For each of the environmental scenarios below, sketch a supply curve to illustrate and explain the change.

**a** An erupting volcano sending ash into the sky, causing air travel to come to a stand-still. The flight disruption costs more than US$4 billion.

**b** A firm decides to use solar power, which decreases costs of production in the long term, meaning that the firm is willing and able to increase supply, producing more at that same price when it becomes more profitable to do so.

ISBN: 9780170241946

c A coal mining company restores land to its pre-mining condition (apart from the missing coal).

d A trucking company invests in tree plantations in order to offset their carbon emissions.

e A firm decides to lower its costs of production by using more time- and energy-efficient measures to lower the cost of trashing and recycling its waste.

f A restaurant chooses to use only organic ingredients, which are more expensive.

**3**

Page 99

**17** Identify two laws that might affect the supply decisions of a business.

_____

_____

**18** Identify one law, or law change, that may increase supply.

_____

**19** For each of the legal requirement scenarios below, sketch a supply curve to illustrate and explain the change.

  **a** A clothing store shuts on Good Friday because of the legal requirement outlined in the Shop Trading Hours Act.

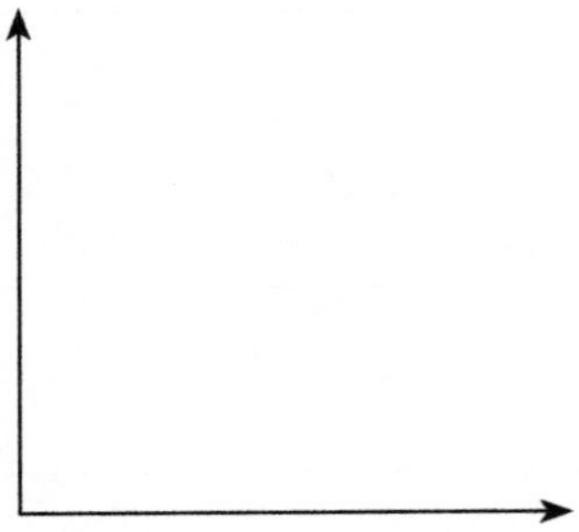

  _____

  _____

  _____

  _____

  _____

  _____

  _____

  _____

  **b** New laws are introduced requiring more detailed labelling of food products.

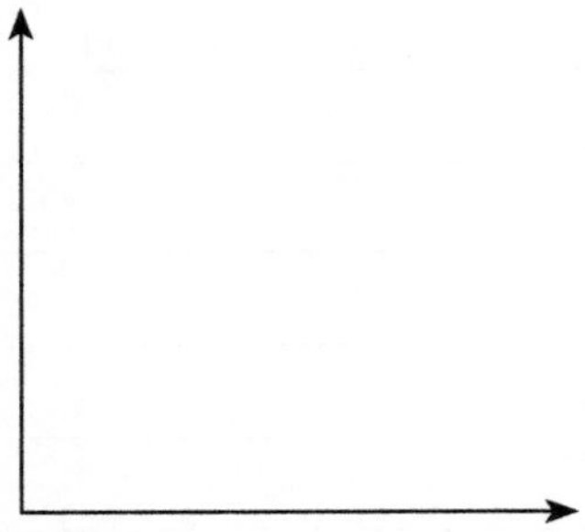

  _____

  _____

  _____

  _____

  _____

  _____

  _____

  **c** New health and safety standards are introduced by law, requiring staff to be issued with new safety gear.

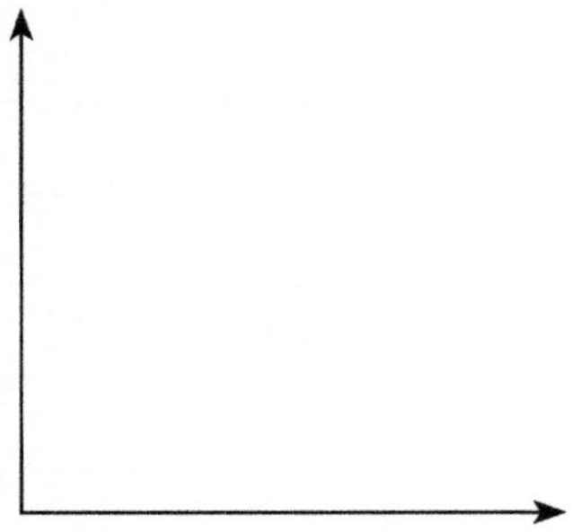

  _____

  _____

  _____

  _____

  _____

  _____

  _____

ISBN: 9780170241946

**d** Staff are required by law to have an extra weeks paid holiday per year.

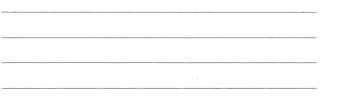

_____
_____
_____
_____
_____
_____
_____

**e** There is an increase in the paid parental leave entitlements.

_____
_____
_____
_____
_____
_____
_____

**20** For each of the political decision scenarios below, sketch a supply curve to illustrate and explain the change.

Page 100

**a** Subsidies are increased for the producers of safety belts.

_____
_____
_____
_____
_____
_____
_____

**b** Sales taxes on cigarettes are increased.

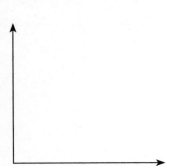

_____
_____
_____
_____
_____
_____

ISBN: 9780170241946

**3**

c   GST is increased to 18.5%

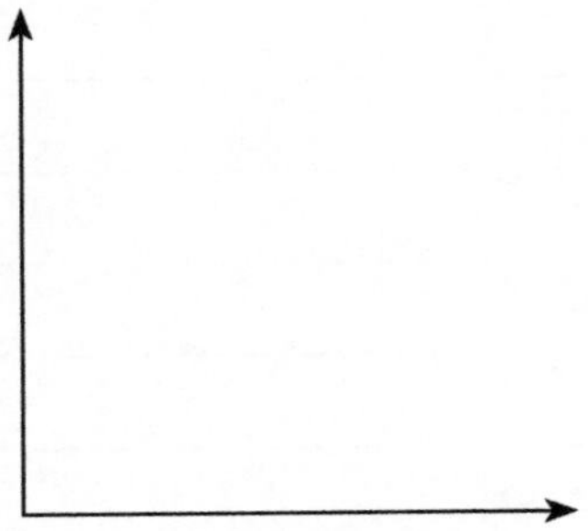

d   The government determines that New Zealand will not import from a particular country because of that country diminishing its citizen's civil rights.

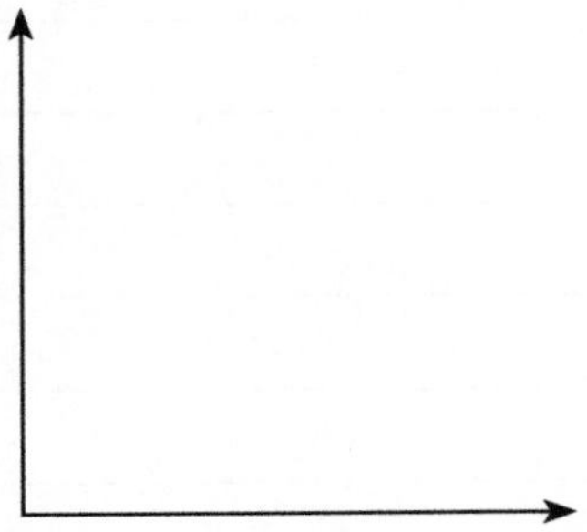

21  Use your research skills to describe what Fair Trade Coffee is. If Mariah's Cafe has strong political feelings about the importance of supporting Fair Trade Coffee, explain how this might affect their supply decisions.

ISBN: 9780170241946

**22** Use a Venn diagram to compare and contrast quotas and tariffs.

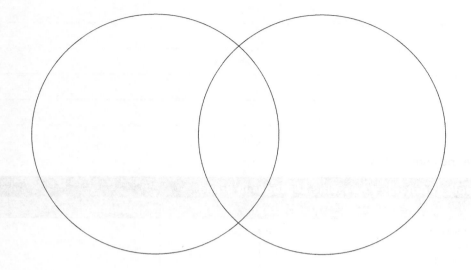

**23** Use the supply model to explain the effect of the following on supply:
  **a** A tariff on imports used in production, is lifted.

_____
_____
_____
_____
_____
_____
_____
_____

  **b** A quota on imports used in production is increased.

_____
_____
_____
_____
_____
_____
_____
_____

**24** Find out the current exchange rate for:

  **a** Aus$ _____

  **b** US$ _____

  **c** Euro _____

ISBN: 9780170241946

**3**

Page 103

**25** Use your research skills to find out what tapu means. Explain how it might affect the supply decisions of a firm.

_____

_____

_____

_____

_____

**26** Complete the chart below.

| The Supply of Antonio's Awesome Sausages in Bread | | | |
|---|---|---|---|
| Scenario | Factor | Graph | Explanation |
| Sausage sizzle attendants to wear fireproof aprons | | 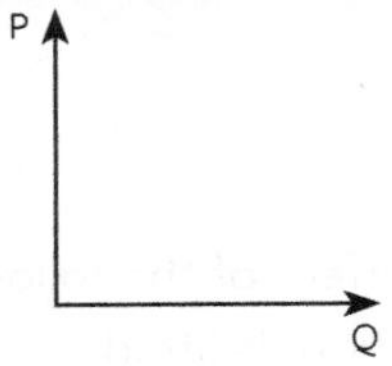 P↑ Q→ | |
| Smoke from sausage sizzles to be reduced and compulsory low smoke burners to be used | | 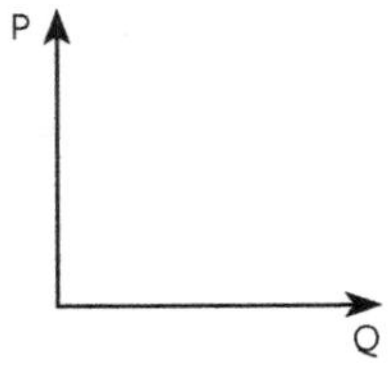 P↑ Q→ | |
| | Cultural obligation | 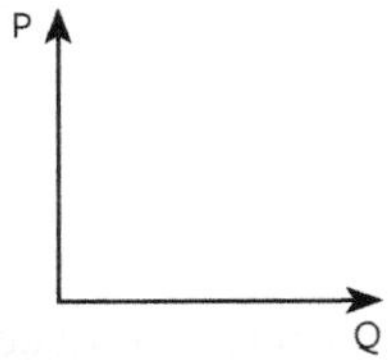 P↑ Q→ | The firm needs a report from the tangata whenua before proceeding with development, increasing costs, decreasing supply, shifting the curve to the left |
| Company taxes rise | | 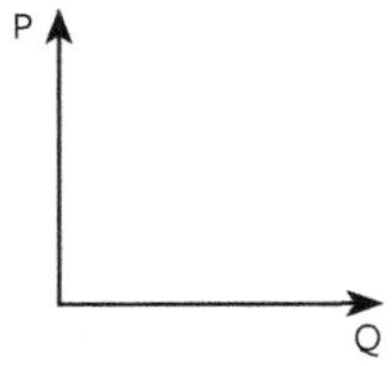 P↑ Q→ | |
| Import taxes on US tomato ketchup removed, lower price of ketchup | | 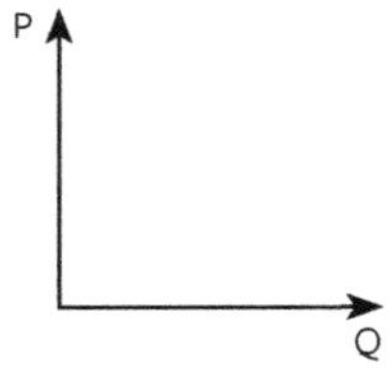 P↑ Q→ | |

ISBN: 9780170241946

# Consumer, producer & government choices using supply and demand

**4**

Exchange Rates

| | We Sell |
|---|---|
| AUSTRALIA | 0.8264 |
| BRAZIL | 0.5263 |
| CANADA | 0.9677 |
| Costa Rica | 0.1417 |
| Euro | 0.0023 |
| | 1.4093 |
| HONG KONG | 0.1412 |
| JAPAN | 0.0094 |
| MEXICO | 0.1014 |
| NEW ZEALAND | 0.7284 |
| S Korea | 0.0012 |
| SINGAPORE | 0.6922 |
| Sweden | 0.1502 |
| Switzerland | 0.8837 |
| TAHITI | 0.0123 |
| TAIWAN | 0.0342 |
| THAILAND | 0.0302 |

1  List ten markets in the table below. Use the images above to help you.

Page 104

2  For each market you have identified, state:
   **a**  Who is the buyer?      **c**  What is the product?
   **b**  Who is the seller?     **d**  Is it a place or a situation?

| | Market | Who is the buyer? | Who is the seller? | What is the product? | Is it a place or a situation? |
|---|---|---|---|---|---|
| 1 | | | | | |
| 2 | | | | | |
| 3 | | | | | |
| 4 | | | | | |
| 5 | | | | | |
| 6 | | | | | |
| 7 | | | | | |
| 8 | | | | | |
| 9 | | | | | |
| 10 | | | | | |

ISBN: 9780170241946

**3** Describe a transaction.

_____

_____

_____

**4** Define a market.

_____

_____

_____

**Page 106**

**5** Identify a possible market for each of these businesses:

*Countdown* _____

*Hoyts Cinema* _____

*Tuckers Panelbeaters* _____

*PioPio Plumbers* _____

*Sony* _____

*Slingshot* _____

**6** Assess these three students' definitions of a market and answer the questions that follow.

**Sophie**

A market is a place where buyers and sellers can communicate and exchange goods and services.

A market is where buyers and sellers meet to exchange goods or services.

**Fergus**

**Coco**

A market is a place or situation where goods and services are exchanged.

**a** Identify the best answer. _____

**b** Explain what this answer has that the other answers do not have.

_____

_____

_____

_____

**c** Are there any other details that this student could have included.

_____

_____

**Page 107**

**7** Distinguish between individual supply and market supply.

_____

_____

_____

ISBN: 9780170241946

**8** Distinguish between individual demand and market demand.

_____

_____

_____

## The lemonade stand

Let us consider the market demand for homemade lemonade for sale in Lucy's front yard. There are three people who are willing and able to buy lemonade: Dad, Nana and Lucy's big brother Darius. (Baby Noni is willing to buy but has no money, so cannot be included in our market demand.)

Page 108–110

The individual demand schedules and demand curves for Dad, Nana and Darius are shown below:

| Dad's Daily Demand Schedule for Homemade Lemonade | |
|---|---|
| Price ($) | Quantity (glasses) |
| 1 | 3 |
| 2 | 2 |
| 3 | 1 |

| Nana's Daily Demand Schedule for Homemade Lemonade | |
|---|---|
| Price ($) | Quantity (glasses) |
| 1 | 4 |
| 2 | 3 |
| 3 | 2 |

| Darius' Daily Demand Schedule for Homemade Lemonade | |
|---|---|
| Price ($) | Quantity (glasses) |
| 1 | 2 |
| 2 | 1 |
| 3 | 0 |

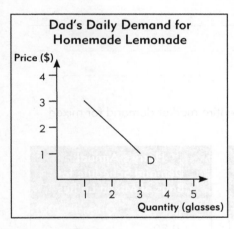

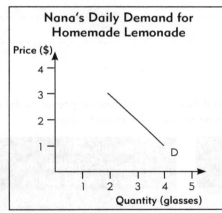

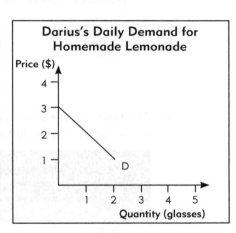

How do we explain the information taken from these tables and graphs?

Dad will demand:
- 3 glasses a day when the price is $1
- 2 glasses a day when the price is $2
- 1 glass a day when the price is $3

Nana will demand:
- 4 glasses a day when the price is $1
- 3 glasses a day when the price is $2
- 2 glasses a day when the price is $3

Darius will demand:
- 2 glasses a day when the price is $1
- 1 glass a day when the price is $2
- 0 glasses a day when the price is $3

In total, therefore, if the price is $1 the market (all buyers: Dad, Nana and Darius) will demand:
3 + 4 + 2 = 9 glasses of lemonade per day.

If the price is $2 the market (all buyers: Dad, Nana and Darius) will demand:
2 + 3 + 1 = 6 glasses of lemonade per day.

If the price is $3 the market (all buyers: Dad, Nana and Darius) will demand:
1 + 2 + 0 = 3 glasses of lemonade per day.

ISBN: 9780170241946

We can use this information to create a **Market Demand Schedule**.

**The Daily Market Demand Schedule for Homemade Lemonade**

| Price ($) | Quantity (glasses) |
|-----------|--------------------|
| 1 | 9 |
| 2 | 6 |
| 3 | 3 |

From this table we can plot a **Market Demand Curve**.

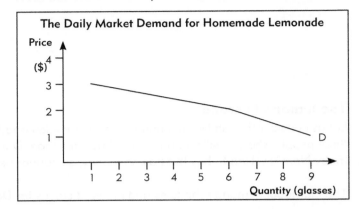

**9** Using the case study above:

**a** Explain why the market demand curve is the horizontal summation of individual demand curves.

_____

_____

_____

**b** Explain why prices have remained the same in the market demand curve as they were in the individual demand curves.

_____

_____

_____

**10** The following set of individual demand schedules represents the entire market demand for mixed lollies. Graph the market demand curve for mixed lollies.

| Emelia's Annual Demand Schedule for Bags of Mixed Lollies | |
|---------------------------------------------------------|--|
| Price ($) | Quantity (00) |
| 0.50 | 10 |
| 0.60 | 8 |
| 0.70 | 6 |
| 0.80 | 4 |
| 0.90 | 2 |
| 1.00 | 1 |

| Niamh's Annual Demand Schedule for Bags of Mixed Lollies | |
|--------------------------------------------------------|--|
| Price ($) | Quantity (00) |
| 0.50 | 12 |
| 0.60 | 11 |
| 0.70 | 10 |
| 0.80 | 9 |
| 0.90 | 8 |
| 1.00 | 7 |

| Harry's Annual Demand Schedule for Bags of Mixed Lollies | |
|--------------------------------------------------------|--|
| Price ($) | Quantity (00) |
| 0.50 | 6 |
| 0.60 | 5 |
| 0.70 | 4 |
| 0.80 | 3 |
| 0.90 | 2 |
| 1.00 | 1 |

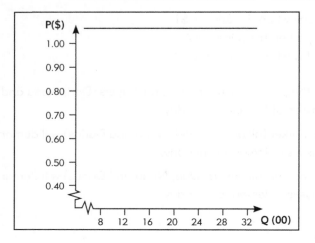

ISBN: 9780170241946

**11** The following individual demands represent the entire market demand for gymnastic lessons. Graph the market demand for gymnastic lessons per year.

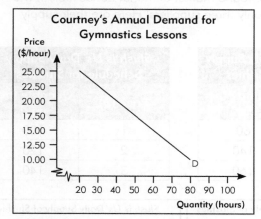

| Danielle's Annual Demand Schedule for Gymnastic Lessons ||
|---|---|
| Price ($/hour) | Quantity (hours) |
| 25.00 | 70 |
| 22.50 | 75 |
| 20.00 | 80 |
| 17.50 | 85 |
| 15.00 | 90 |
| 12.50 | 95 |
| 10.00 | 100 |

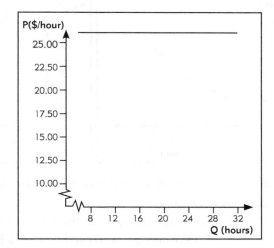

**12** Room 16 at Oranga Primary are selling cookies to raise funds for a camp. In week 1 the cookies were $1, the junior school bought 20, the middle school bought 23 and the senior school bought 15. Room 16 thought they could raise more funds if they doubled the price in week 2. The juniors bought 15, the middle school bought 18 and the seniors bought 10. Room 16 increased the price in week 3 to $3, and sold 3 to the juniors, 8 to the middle school and 1 to the seniors.

**a** Prepare the market demand schedule for cookie sales at Oranga Primary.

**b** Graph the market demand curve for cookie sales at Oranga Primary.

Page 111–113

## Market supply

We can find market supply in much the same way that we found market demand. Let us look at the supply of slushies in Ashburton, assuming that there are only three suppliers. Here are their supply schedules and supply curves:

| *Slushman's* Daily Supply Schedule for Slushies | |
|---|---|
| Price ($) | Quantity (per day) |
| 1 | 40 |
| 2 | 120 |
| 3 | 160 |

| *Slushmaestro's* Daily Supply Schedule for Slushies | |
|---|---|
| Price ($) | Quantity (per day) |
| 1 | 60 |
| 2 | 140 |
| 3 | 160 |

| *Slush is Us'* Daily Supply Schedule for Slushies | |
|---|---|
| Price ($) | Quantity (per day) |
| 1 | 100 |
| 2 | 120 |
| 3 | 140 |

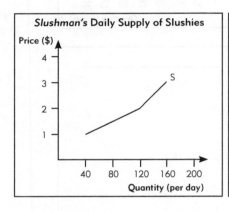
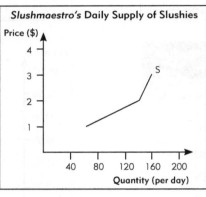
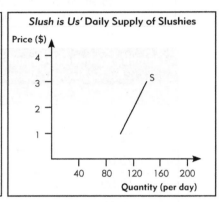

How do we explain the information taken from these tables and graphs?

*Slushman* will supply:
- 40 slushies a day when the price is $1
- 120 slushies a day when the price is $2
- 160 slushies a day when the price is $3

*Slushmaestro* will supply:
- 60 slushies a day when the price is $1
- 140 slushies a day when the price is $2
- 160 slushies a day when the price is $3

*Slush is Us* will supply:
- 100 slushies a day when the price is $1
- 120 slushies a day when the price is $2
- 140 slushies a day when the price is $3

In total, therefore, if the price is $1 the market (all suppliers: *Slushman, Slushmaestro* and *Slush is Us*) will supply:

40 + 60 + 100 = 200 slushies per day.

If the price is $2 the market (all suppliers: Slushman, Slushmaestro and Slush is Us) will supply:

120 + 140 + 120 = 380 slushies per day.

If the price is $3 the market (all suppliers: Slushman, Slushmaestro and Slush is Us) will supply:

160 + 160 + 140 = 460 slushies per day.

We can use this information to create a market supply schedule.

| The Daily Market Supply Schedule for Slushies in Ashburton | |
|---|---|
| Price ($) | Quantity (per day) |
| 1 | 200 |
| 2 | 380 |
| 3 | 400 |

And from this schedule we can plot a market supply curve.

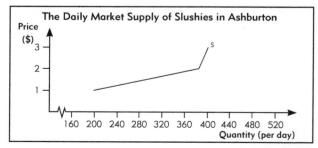

ISBN: 9780170241946

**13** Using the case study above:

**a** Explain why the market supply curve is the horizontal summation of individual supply curves.

_____

_____

_____

**b** Explain why prices have remained the same in the market supply curve as they were in the individual supply curves.

_____

_____

_____

**14** Use the following individual supply schedules to create a market supply schedule and market supply curve for lollipops.

| Cory's Corner Dairy Weekly Supply Schedule for Lollipops | |
|---|---|
| Price ($) | Quantity (boxes) |
| 4 | 9 |
| 6 | 12 |
| 8 | 15 |

| Mitzi's Mid-Street Dairy Weekly Supply Schedule for Lollipops | |
|---|---|
| Price ($) | Quantity (boxes) |
| 4 | 18 |
| 6 | 20 |
| 8 | 26 |

| Dinesh's Downtown Dairy Weekly Supply Schedule for Lollipops | |
|---|---|
| Price ($) | Quantity (boxes) |
| 4 | 8 |
| 6 | 11 |
| 8 | 19 |

| The Weekly Market Supply Schedule for Lollipops | |
|---|---|
| Price ($) | Quantity (boxes) |
| 4 | |
| 6 | |
| 8 | |

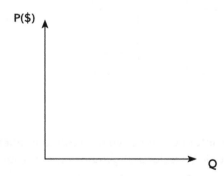

**15** Use the following individual supply curves to create a market supply schedule and market supply curve for eggs.

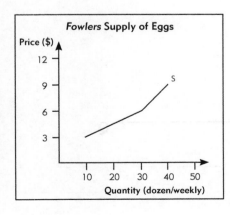

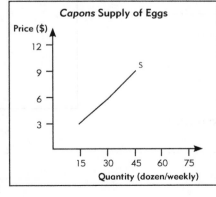

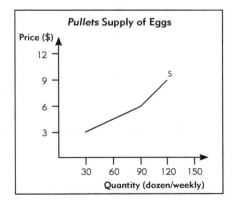

ISBN: 9780170241946

4

| Price ($) | Quantity (dozen/weekly) |
|-----------|-------------------------|
|           |                         |
|           |                         |
|           |                         |
|           |                         |

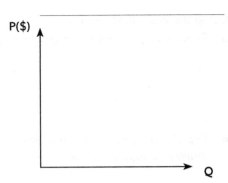

16 Compare the market demand for lollipops in question 2 and the market supply for eggs in question 3. Outline how the time frame can be shown in a demand schedule or a demand curve.

_____

_____

_____

17 There are three gymnasiums in Tauranga. They all offer pre-season conditioning for rugby players. Foster's Gym offered one training session a week at $5 per session, three training sessions per week at $10 per session, six at $15 per session and at $20 per session they offer a session every day.

| Dean's Weekly Supply of Preconditioning Sessions | |
|---------------------|---------------------|
| Price ($) | Quantity (weekly) |
| 5 | 1 |
| 10 | 2 |
| 15 | 3 |
| 20 | 5 |

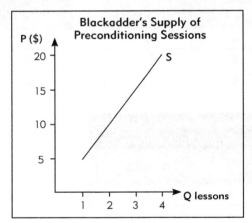

Use all the information above to create a market demand schedule and a market supply curve for preconditioning sessions at gymnasiums in Tauranga.

| Price ($) | Quantity (weekly) |
|-----------|-------------------|
| 5 | |
| 10 | |
| 15 | |
| 20 | |

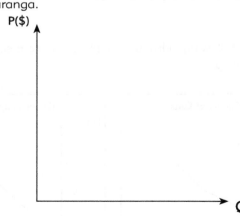

Page 116–117

18 Explain how a market reacts to a shortage.

_____

_____

_____

_____

_____

ISBN: 9780170241946

**19** Explain how a market responds to a surplus.

_____

_____

_____

_____

_____

**20** Use _TradeMe_ as an example to explain why consumers raise prices when they want to buy things as cheaply as possible.

_____

_____

_____

_____

**21** Explain why a producer would lower prices when they can make larger profits at higher prices.

_____

_____

_____

_____

**22** Plot the following figures accurately on a graph and derive the market price, then answer the questions that follow. Ensure your diagram is fully labelled and clearly identify equilibrium price (Pe) and equilibrium quantity (Qe).

| Market for Milk | | |
|---|---|---|
| Price ($/litre) | Quantity demanded (million litres) | Quantity supplied (million litres) |
| 3.95 | 75 | 15 |
| 3.96 | 70 | 20 |
| 3.97 | 65 | 25 |
| 3.98 | 60 | 30 |
| 3.99 | 55 | 35 |
| 4.00 | 50 | 40 |
| 4.01 | 45 | 45 |
| 4.02 | 40 | 50 |
| 4.03 | 35 | 60 |
| 4.04 | 30 | 65 |
| 4.05 | 25 | 70 |
| 4.06 | 20 | 75 |
| 4.07 | 15 | 80 |

**4**

a   Describe the situation that would arise if the suppliers made an error and charged a price above the equilibrium price you have derived. Show this on your graph and explain in words the sequence of events that would follow.

_____

_____

_____

_____

b   If the price of milk was set below your market price, describe the situation that would arise. Explain in words the sequence of events that would follow.

_____

_____

_____

_____

23  Match the terms in column A with the correct definition in column B in the grid below.

| Column A | | Column B | |
|---|---|---|---|
| 1 | equilibrium price | a | the graph that shows the quantities that will be produced at a range of prices, *ceteris paribus* |
| 2 | non-equilibrium prices | b | an excess of demand |
| 3 | shortage | c | the providers of goods and services |
| 4 | surplus | d | prices where there is pressure to change |
| 5 | market forces | e | pressure within the market to move to the equilibrium point |
| 6 | consumers | f | an excess of supply |
| 7 | producers | g | a table that shows the quantities that will be bought at a range of prices, *ceteris paribus* |
| 8 | demand schedule | h | the price at which the quantity supplied equals the quantity demanded |
| 9 | supply curve | i | the users of goods and services |

| | |
|---|---|
| 1 | |
| 2 | |
| 3 | |
| 4 | |
| 5 | |
| 6 | |
| 7 | |
| 8 | |
| 9 | |

24  Plot the market diagram from the schedules below and answer the questions that follow. Clearly identify equilibrium price (Pe) and equilibrium quantity (Qe) on your graph.

| Market Demand Schedule for Apricots | |
|---|---|
| Price ($) | Quantity (000 kg) |
| 1.00 | 18 |
| 1.10 | 17 |
| 1.20 | 16 |
| 1.30 | 15 |
| 1.40 | 14 |
| 1.50 | 13 |
| 1.60 | 12 |
| 1.70 | 11 |

| Market Supply Schedule for Apricots | |
|---|---|
| Price ($) | Quantity (000 kg) |
| 1.00 | 10 |
| 1.10 | 11 |
| 1.20 | 12 |
| 1.30 | 13 |
| 1.40 | 14 |
| 1.50 | 15 |
| 1.60 | 16 |
| 1.70 | 17 |

ISBN: 9780170241946

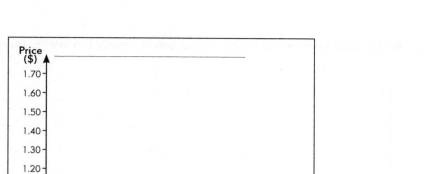

**a** Explain what would happen if the producers decided to sell their apricots at $1.10/kg.

_____

_____

_____

_____

_____

**b** Explain what would happen if producers decided to sell their apricots at $1.70/kg.

_____

_____

_____

_____

_____

**c** Using your answers to the previous two questions, explain why the market will eventually operate at $1.40/kg.

_____

_____

_____

_____

_____

**25** Use the supply and demand model to show the effect of:

**a** A decrease in income on chuck steak (an inferior good).

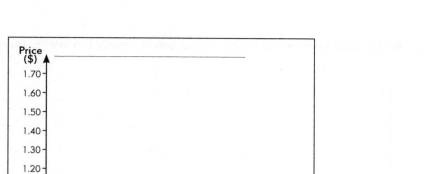

_____

_____

_____

_____

_____

_____

Page 122

ISBN: 9780170241946

**b** An increase in income on supermarket brand cereals (an inferior brand).

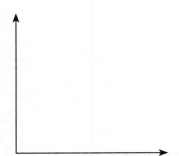

**26** Use the supply and demand model to show the effect of:
  **a** The market for ice blocks as the weather gets colder.

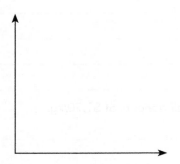

**b** The market for quiche after it is found that eggs are the new superfood.

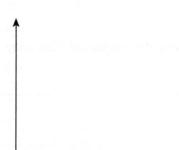

**27** Use the supply and demand model to show the effect of:
  **a** The market for netball shoes in winter.

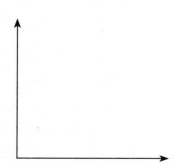

ISBN: 9780170241946

**b** The release of a huge new teen movie on the sale of movie-related merchandise.

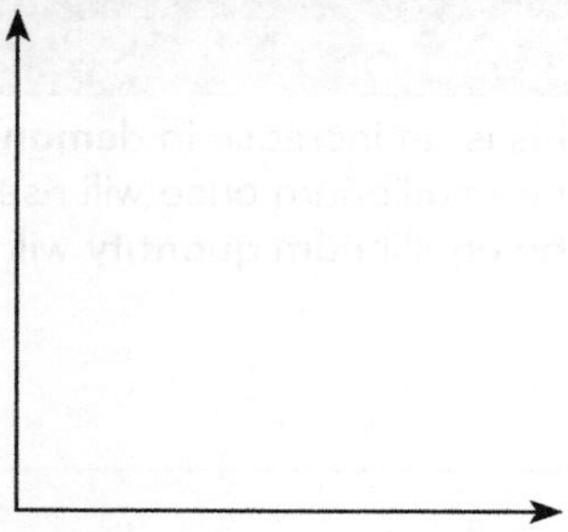

_____

_____

_____

_____

_____

_____

**28** Complete the following chart.

Page 123–124

| The Market for Pies | | | |
|---|---|---|---|
| **Scenario** | **Factor** | **Graph** | **Explanation** |
| Traditional Kiwi food becomes the next big food fad | Taste and preferences have moved toward the product | 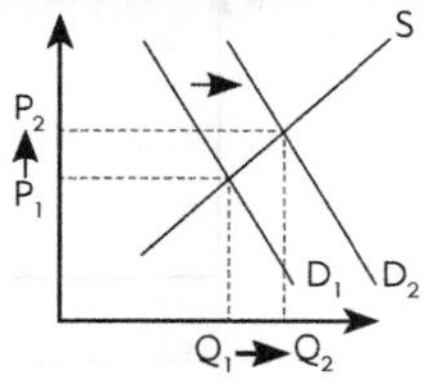 | This is an increase in demand<br>The equilibrium price will rise<br>The equilibrium quantity will rise |
| Tomato sauce falls in price | | 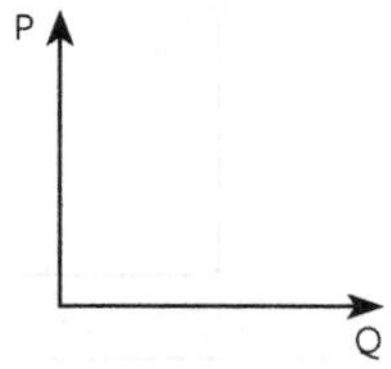 | |
| Huge obesity awareness campaign blames New Zealanders weight problems on our love of pies | | 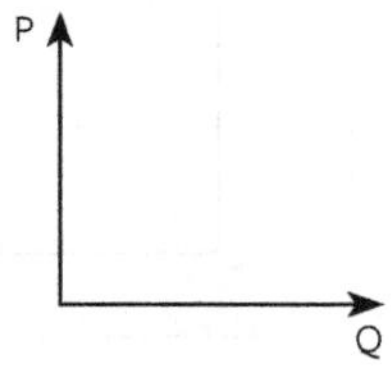 | |
| Pies are an inferior good. Household incomes fall in a period of rising unemployment | | 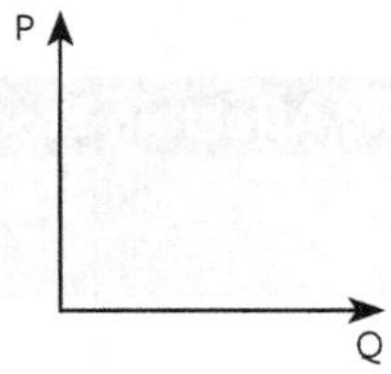 | |
| | Price of a substitute good or service rises | 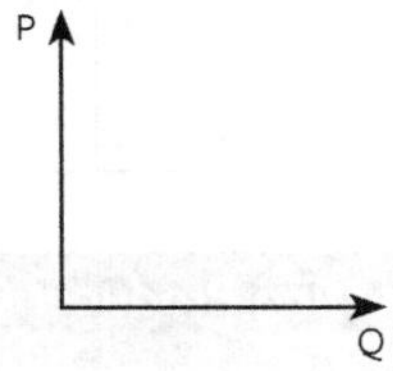 | |

**29** Complete the following chart.

| The Market for Coffee | | | |
|---|---|---|---|
| **Scenario** | **Factor** | **Graph** | **Explanation** |
| Hot chocolate rises in price | | 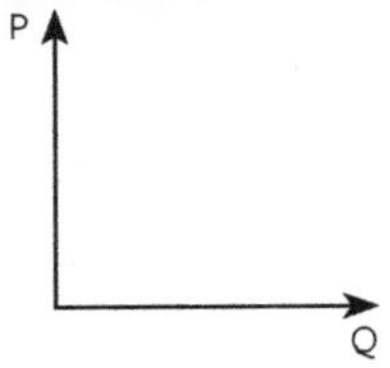 P ↑ → Q | This is an increase in **demand** The equilibrium price will rise The equilibrium **quantity** will rise |
| Biscotti falls in price | | 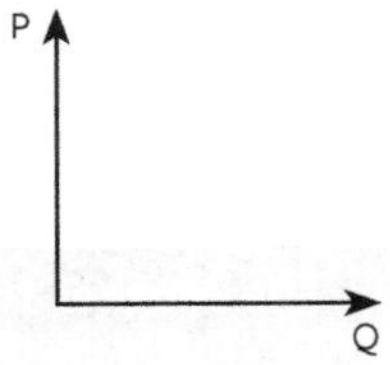 P ↑ → Q | |
| | Incomes fall | 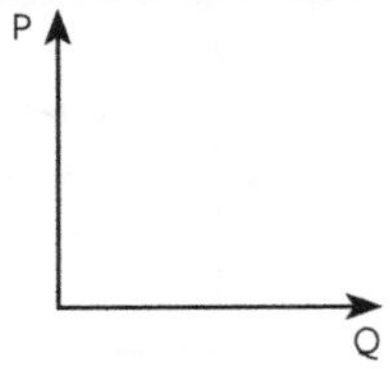 P ↑ → Q | |
| | Price of a substitute rises | 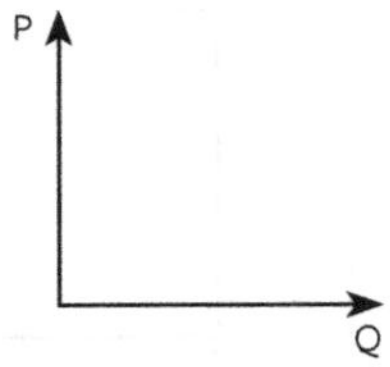 P ↑ → Q | |
| Coffee linked to heart disease | | 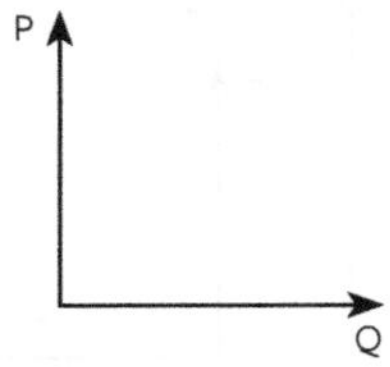 P ↑ → Q | |

Page 125

**30** Complete the following chart.

| Factors Affecting Producer Choices | | | |
|---|---|---|---|
| Changes in the price of other goods | Changes in costs of production | Changes in technology | Changes in productivity |
| | | | |

| Factors Affecting Producer Choices (continued) | | | | |
|---|---|---|---|---|
| Trade | Legal | Environment | Political | Cultural obligations |
| | | | | |

ISBN: 9780170241946

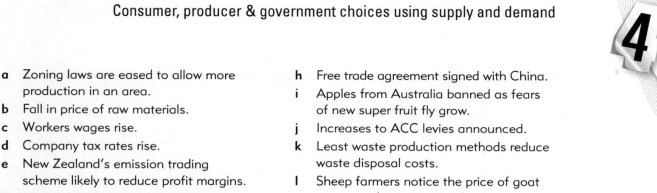

a   Zoning laws are eased to allow more production in an area.

b   Fall in price of raw materials.

c   Workers wages rise.

d   Company tax rates rise.

e   New Zealand's emission trading scheme likely to reduce profit margins.

f   Mining mad legal in national parks.

g   New nano-technology revolutionises manufacturing processes.

h   Free trade agreement signed with China.

i   Apples from Australia banned as fears of new super fruit fly grow.

j   Increases to ACC levies announced.

k   Least waste production methods reduce waste disposal costs.

l   Sheep farmers notice the price of goat carcasses have increased.

m   Iwi tighten up regarding Resource Management Act considerations.

31 a   Identify examples of each of the factors affecting producer choices for each of the following production processes.

   i   Sheep farming
   
   • improvements in technology

   _____

   _____

   _____

   • increases in the prices of other goods

   _____

   _____

   _____

   ii   Fast food takeaways

   • negative impact of environmental factor

   _____

   _____

   _____

   • positive political factor

   _____

   _____

   _____

   iii   Mussel farming (aquaculture)

   • negative impact of cultural factor

   _____

   _____

   _____

   • fall in costs of production

   _____

   _____

   _____

**b** For each of the examples you identified, explain the impact the factor has on the market.

    **i**    Sheep farming
- improvements in technology

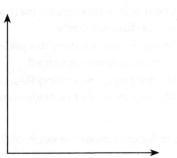

_____

_____

_____

_____

_____

_____

_____

- increases in the prices of other goods

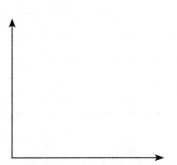

_____

_____

_____

_____

_____

_____

_____

_____

    **ii**   Fast food takeaways
- negative impact of environmental factor

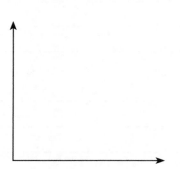

_____

_____

_____

_____

_____

_____

_____

- positive political factor

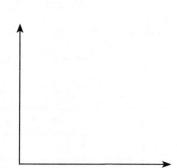

_____

_____

_____

_____

_____

_____

_____

ISBN: 9780170241946

iii  Mussel farming (aquaculture)
- negative impact of cultural factor

- fall in costs of production

32  Complete the following chart concerning a firm that produces paper.

Page 127–130

| Scenario | Factor | Graph | Explanation |
|---|---|---|---|
| Cost of wood chip falls (used to make paper) | Wood chips is an input into the paper making process. This is a decrease in cost of production | P, S, S₁, Pe, Pe₁, Qe, Qe₁, Q | This is an increase in supply. The equilibrium price will decrease. The equilibrium quantity will rise. |
| Compressed wood pulp logs (something you could make instead of paper) rise in price | | P, Q | |
| New pulp making machines speed up paper making process | | P, Q | |
| Firms face fines for toxic waste spill | | P, Q | |

| Scenario | Factor | Graph | Explanation |
|---|---|---|---|
| | Change in legal factor | P↑ Q→ | This is an increase in supply ... |

**33** Complete the following chart concerning the market for banana milkshakes.

| Scenario | Graph | Explanation |
|---|---|---|
| The price of milkshake flavourings rise | P↑ $S_1$ S ← $Pe_1$ Pe D Q $Qe_1$ Qe → | Milkshake flavourings are an example of the costs of production. If costs of production rise then the supply decreases (*shifts to the left*). This causes the equilibrium price to rise and the equilibrium quantity to fall |
| The price of milkshake paper cups falls | P↑ Q→ | |
| A new improved milkshake making machine is available on the market | P↑ Q→ | |
| Import quotas on milkshake thickenings are imposed | P↑ Q→ | |
| New hygiene laws insist all handlers of milk products wear gloves | P↑ Q→ | |
| The price of smoothies rises. Milkshake producers have the resources to produce smoothies | P↑ Q→ | |

ISBN: 9780170241946

**34** Complete the chart below. You will need to identify whether it is a supply factor or a demand factor that is affected.

| The Product is Doughnuts | | | |
|---|---|---|---|
| **Scenario** | **Factor** | **Graph** | **Explanation** |
| Doughnuts are discovered to be a health food | Demand, because tastes and preferences move toward doughnuts | *(graph: P vs Q, supply S, demand shifting right D to D₁, Pe to Pe₁, Qe to Qe₁)* | This is an increase in demand The equilibrium price will rise The equilibrium quantity will rise |
| Sugar for coating doughnuts falls in price | | *(graph: P vs Q)* | |
| Coffee (for drinking your doughnut rises in price | | *(graph: P vs Q)* | |
| The oil that doughnuts are fried in rises in price | | *(graph: P vs Q)* | |
| | Price of a substitute rises | *(graph: P vs Q)* | |
| | | *(graph: P vs Q)* | This is an increase in *supply* |
| Heat efficient burners for cooking oil are developed | | *(graph: P vs Q)* | |
| | The price of a good the doughnut maker could also make rises in price | *(graph: P vs Q)* | This is an decrease in *supply* |

ISBN: 9780170241946

| The Product is Doughnuts | | | |
|---|---|---|---|
| Scenario | Factor | Graph | Explanation |
| The price of kofta (deep-fried potato balls), which are also made in a doughnut fryer, falls | | P, Q axes with X graph | |
| | Income falls | P, Q axes with X graph | |
| Doughnuts are featured in a major new fashion advertising campaign | | P, Q axes with X graph | |

35 Complete the following table to show what would happen to the equilibrium price and quantity of woollen jerseys (in the short-term) in each of the scenarios.

| Scenario | Equilibrium price | Equilibrium quantity |
|---|---|---|
| Advertising makes woollen jerseys popular | | |
| Climatic conditions become warmer | | |
| Nylon fibre becomes cheaper | | |
| Wool prices soar | | |

36 Real-life economics: Use supply and demand theory to explain the following events:
- The salaries of accountants continue to rise.

_____

_____

_____

- House rentals are higher in Auckland than Huntly.

_____

_____

_____

- Pinenuts cost $45 per kilogram (which is very expensive!).

_____

_____

_____

ISBN: 9780170241946

- Salaries for shop assistants rise more slowly that salaries for computer experts.

_____

_____

_____

- Gold is expensive and continues to rise.

_____

_____

_____

37  Using the graphs below, explain the effect of the change shown on the equilibrium price and quantity. Fully label the graphs to illustrate your answer.

a   Playstation 4 is released.

**The Market for Playstation 3**

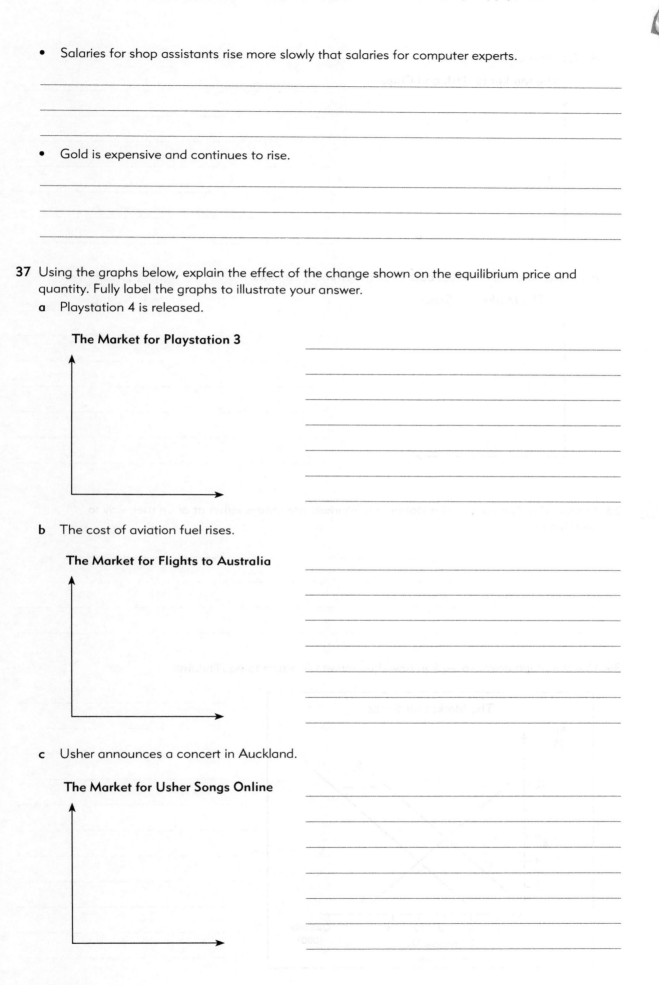

b   The cost of aviation fuel rises.

**The Market for Flights to Australia**

c   Usher announces a concert in Auckland.

**The Market for Usher Songs Online**

ISBN: 9780170241946

**4**

**d** Cooking oil falls in price.

### The Market for Fish and Chips

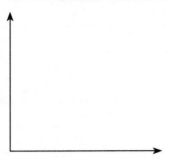

_____
_____
_____
_____
_____
_____
_____

**e** Government announces cuts to all government benefits.

### The Market for Shoes

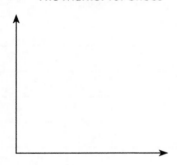

_____
_____
_____
_____
_____
_____
_____
_____

**Page 132–133**

**38** Explain what is meant by the statement, 'Markets are always either at or on their way to equilibrium.'

_____
_____
_____
_____

**39** Use the graph below to explain how the market will return to equilibrium.

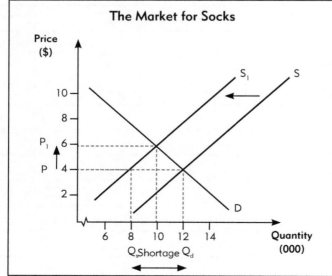

The Market for Socks

_____
_____
_____
_____
_____
_____
_____
_____
_____
_____
_____
_____
_____

ISBN: 9780170241946

_____

_____

_____

_____

_____

**40** Assess the following student responses to question 2 and answer the questions that follow.

**Viliami:** 'The current price is below the equilibrium of $6. This creates a shortage of socks (4000 socks). Consumers cannot get enough socks at this price so they bid the price up. This will cause the quantity demanded to fall and the quantity supplied to rise until quantity demanded equals quantity demanded (10 000 socks) at the equilibrium price of $6, and equilibrium is restored.'

**Kelly:** 'The market forces will force the market to return to equilibrium because this is where supply equals demand and the market is clear.'

**Tama:** 'The price is lower than equilibrium, there is an excess. This excess creates pressure within the market because they want to clear the market so that prices will rise until quantity supplied equals quantity demanded (at 10 000 socks).'

**a** Identify the best answer. _____

**b** Explain what this answer has that the other answers do not have.

_____

_____

_____

_____

**c** Identify any other details that this student could have included.

_____

_____

**41** The table and graph below illustrate the market for chocolate cupcakes. Complete the questions that follow to fully explain market equilibrium in this market.

| Market Demand Schedule for Chocolate Cupcakes | |
|---|---|
| Price ($) | Q (dozen/week) |
| 8.00 | 250 |
| 12.00 | 230 |
| 16.00 | 200 |
| 20.00 | 180 |
| 24.00 | 120 |

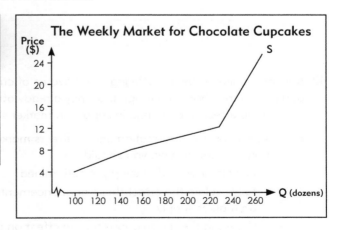

The Weekly Market for Chocolate Cupcakes

**a** Use the graph and the schedule above to:
- complete the market graph by drawing in and labelling the market demand curve
- indicate the market equilibrium price (Pe) and quantity (Qe).

**b** On the graph you drew show the market situation if the price of cupcakes was $20. You must:
- use dotted lines to show the quantity demanded (label this Qd)
- use dotted lines to show the quantity supplied (label this Qs)
- fully label the resulting surplus or shortage.

**c** Discuss how the free market would react to this situation. In your answer, you should:
- fully explain the change in market price
- fully explain the change in quantity demanded and quantity supplied
- refer to the data given.

_____

_____

_____

_____

_____

_____

_____

_____

_____

_____

_____

_____

_____

_____

_____

_____

_____

_____

_____

_____

_____

**42** Recently, bakeries began offering new flavours of cupcakes using all new natural flavourings, in addition to the chocolate range that they already offer. Complete the following questions to fully explain the effect of a change in supply on market equilibrium and consumers.

**a** Discuss how the information above affects market supply. In your answer, you should:
- explain how market supply is determined
- fully explain the effect these announcements have on market supply
- show (on the graph opposite) the effect on the market supply curve, and fully label the change.

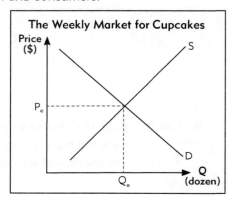

The Weekly Market for Cupcakes

ISBN: 9780170241946

_____

_____

_____

_____

_____

_____

_____

**b** Discuss the effect of this change on the market for cupcakes. In your answer, you should:
- label the new equilibrium quantity and equilibrium price on the graph
- fully explain the effect on consumers of cupcakes.

_____

_____

_____

_____

_____

_____

_____

_____

_____

_____

_____

_____

_____

_____

_____

_____

_____

_____

ISBN: 9780170241946

**43** The table and graph below illustrate the market for snowboards. Complete the questions that follow to fully explain market equilibrium in this market.

| Market Supply Schedule for Snowboards | |
| --- | --- |
| Price ($) | Q (snowboards/ monthly) |
| 500 | 30 |
| 400 | 27 |
| 300 | 20 |
| 200 | 10 |
| 100 | 4 |

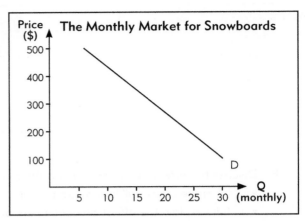

**a** Use the graph and the schedule above to:
- complete the market graph by drawing and labelling the market supply curve
- indicate the market equilibrium price (Pe) and quantity (Qe).

**b** On the graph you drew, show the market situation if the price of snowboards was $200. You must:
- use dotted lines to show the quantity demanded (label this Qd)
- use dotted lines to show the quantity supplied (label this Qs)
- fully label the resulting surplus or shortage.

**c** Discuss how the free market would react to this situation. In your answer, you should:
- fully explain the change in market price
- fully explain the change in quantity demanded and quantity supplied
- refer to the data given.

_____

_____

_____

_____

_____

_____

_____

_____

_____

_____

_____

_____

_____

_____

_____

_____

_____

_____

_____

_____

ISBN: 9780170241946

Page 137–138

**44** 'Consumers are choosing Fair Trade coffee over non-Fair Trade coffee. Fair Trade sales grew by 72% in New Zealand' (Source: www.fta.org.au). Use the graph below to answer the questions that follow.

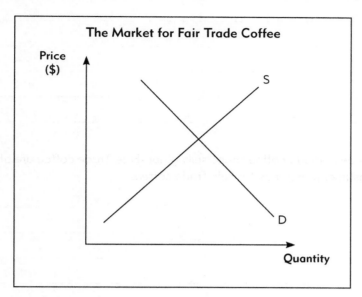

**The Market for Fair Trade Coffee**

**a** Explain what is meant by the term 'Fair Trade'.

_____

_____

**b** Show the effect of increased consumer preference for Fair Trade coffee on your graph. Label all changes.

**c** Explain how the market will restore equilibrium following the change you have shown.

_____

_____

_____

_____

_____

**d** List all the individuals of groups affected by changes in the Fair Trade coffee market. (Hint: Brainstorm!)

Groups affected by changes in Fair Trade Coffee Market

ISBN: 9780170241946

**e**   Explain how Fair Trade coffee bean farmers are affected by the increased consumer preference for Fair Trade coffee.

_____

_____

_____

_____

_____

**f**   Explain how New Zealand coffee shops selling non-Free Trade coffee are affected by the increased consumer preference for Fair Trade coffee.

_____

_____

_____

_____

_____

**45**  Transport Minister: 'It will be illegal for drivers to talk or send text messages on handheld mobile devices while driving from November 1 [2009]'. (Source: www.nzherald.co.nz) Use the graph below to answer the questions that follow.

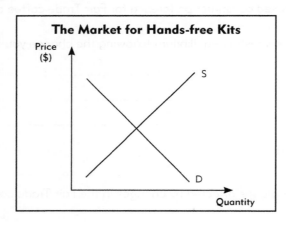

**a**   Show the effect of the mobile phone restriction on the market for hands-free kits for motor vehicles on your graph. Label all changes.

**b**   Explain how the market will restore equilibrium following the change you have shown.

_____

_____

_____

_____

_____

ISBN: 9780170241946

c   List all the individuals or groups affected by changes in the mobile phone market. (Hint: Brainstorm!)

d   Explain how mobile service providers will be affected by the ban on hand-held mobile phone use in cars.

_____

_____

_____

_____

_____

e   Explain how employees of hands-free kit manufacturers may be affected by the ban of using hand-held mobile devices while driving.

_____

_____

_____

_____

_____

46  New anti-pollution regulations by the Bay of Plenty District Council has made it necessary for dairy farmers to get a council-certified effluent drainage check yearly.

a   Show the effect of the new regulations on the market for milk on the graph. Fully label your changes

b   Discuss how the free market would react to this situation. In your answer, you should:
   •   fully explain the change in market price
   •   fully explain the change in quantity demanded and quantity supplied
   •   fully explain the impact of the new regulations:
      o   on dairy farmers' profits
      o   on consumers.

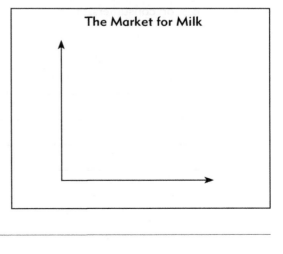

The Market for Milk

_____

_____

_____

_____

ISBN: 9780170241946

_____
_____
_____
_____
_____
_____
_____
_____
_____
_____
_____
_____
_____
_____
_____
_____
_____

**47** Compact disc (CD) recordings of music are to be phased out – music will only be available online.

  **a**  Show the effect of the phasing out CDs on the market for MP3 Players on the graph below. Fully label your changes.

  **b**  Discuss how the free market would react to this situation. In your answer, you should:
  - fully explain the change in market price
  - fully explain the change in quantity demanded and quantity supplied
  - fully explain the impact of the phasing out of CDs:
    - o   on music stores
    - o   on consumers.

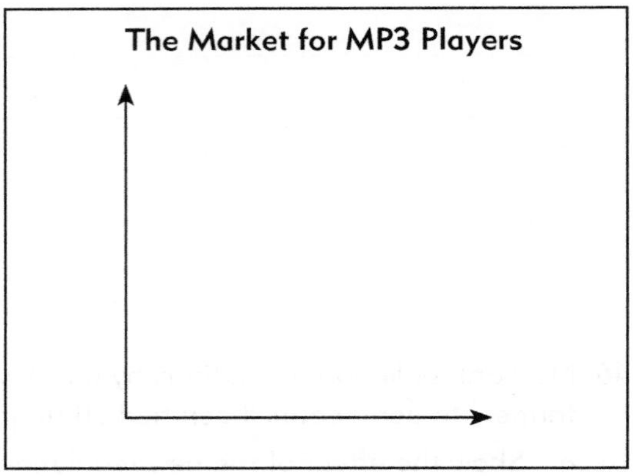

**The Market for MP3 Players**

_____
_____
_____
_____
_____
_____
_____
_____
_____
_____
_____
_____

ISBN: 9780170241946

48 Use the following market demand and supply schedules to plot the market for cycle helmets diagram and use it to answer the questions that follow.

Page 141

| Market Demand Schedule for Cycle Helmets | |
|---|---|
| Price ($) | Quantity (monthly) |
| 100 | 1000 |
| 90 | 1200 |
| 80 | 1400 |
| 70 | 1600 |
| 60 | 1800 |
| 50 | 2000 |
| 40 | 2200 |
| 30 | 2400 |

| Market Supply Schedule for Cycle Helmets | |
|---|---|
| Price ($) | Quantity (monthly) |
| 100 | 2800 |
| 90 | 2400 |
| 80 | 2000 |
| 70 | 1600 |
| 60 | 1200 |
| 50 | 800 |
| 40 | 400 |
| 30 | 100 |

**The Market for Cycle Helmets**

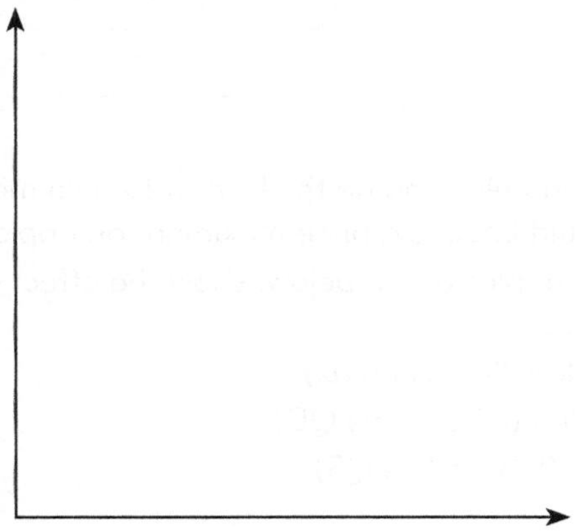

a   Clearly show and label a price maximum of $50 on your diagram.

b   Clearly show and label the excess generated by the price maximum.

c   Calculate the size of the excess

Excess = _____ monthly

d   Explain why the market does not clear.

_____

_____

_____

e   Calculate the total sales at market equilibrium.

$ _____

f   Calculate the total sales after the price maximum was imposed.

$ _____

g   Explain why the government would impose a price maximum.

_____

_____

_____

_____

h   Use your answers to e and f to outline how successful this strategy has been in achieving the government's goal.

_____

_____

_____

_____

i   Explain what would happen if the government changed the price maximum to $100.

_____

_____

**49** Carlos has been studying Economics and he thinks that to help make healthy food more affordable perhaps the government should impose a price maximum on apples.

a   On the weekly market for apples graph below, show the effect of a maximum price control at $1.80. You must include:
   •   the maximum price (labelled as Pmax)
   •   the quantity demanded (labelled as QD)
   •   the quantity supplied (labelled as QS).

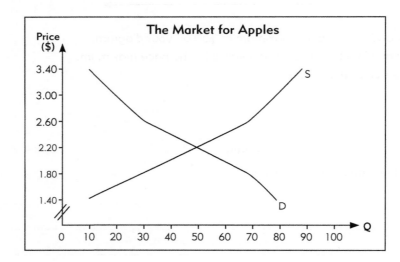

ISBN: 9780170241946

**b** Referring to your graph above, fully explain the consequences of a maximum price control on the market for apples. Include the following in your explanation:
  * quantity demanded before AND after the maximum price control
  * quantity supplied before AND after the maximum price control
  * a problem the maximum price control might create
  * a possible solution for the above problem.

_____

_____

_____

_____

_____

_____

_____

_____

_____

_____

_____

_____

_____

_____

_____

_____

_____

_____

_____

_____

_____

_____

_____

**50** Use the following market demand and supply schedule to plot the market for pre-mixed alcoholic drinks and use it to answer the questions that follow.

Page 143

| Market Demand Schedule for Pre-mixed Alcoholic Drinks, per Week | |
| --- | --- |
| Price ($) | Quantity (can) |
| 10.00 | 325 |
| 9.50 | 350 |
| 9.00 | 375 |
| 8.50 | 400 |
| 8.00 | 425 |
| 7.50 | 450 |
| 7.00 | 475 |

| Market Supply Schedule for Pre-mixed Alcoholic Drinks, per Week | |
| --- | --- |
| Price ($) | Quantity (can) |
| 10.00 | 475 |
| 9.50 | 450 |
| 9.00 | 425 |
| 8.50 | 400 |
| 8.00 | 375 |
| 7.50 | 350 |
| 7.00 | 325 |

ISBN: 9780170241946

## The Market for Pre-mixed Alcoholic Drinks

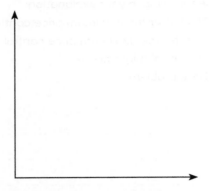

a   Clearly show and label a price minimum of $9.50 on your diagram.

b   Clearly show and label the excess generated by the price minimum.

c   Calculate the size of the excess

Excess = _____ cans

d   Explain why the market does not clear.

_____

_____

_____

e   Calculate the total sales at market equilibrium.

$ _____

f   Calculate the total sales after the price minimum was imposed.

$ _____

g   Explain why the government would impose a price minimum.

_____

_____

_____

_____

h   Use your answers to e and f to outline how successful their strategy has been.

_____

_____

_____

_____

ISBN: 9780170241946

**i** Explain what would happen if the government changed the price minimum to $7.50.

_____

_____

**51** The government is concerned about young people smoking and has decided to impose a price minimum on cigarettes.

**a** On the weekly market for cigarettes graph below, show the effect of a minimum price control at $2.50. You must include:
- the maximum price (labelled as Pmin)
- the quantity demanded (labelled as QD)
- the quantity supplied (labelled as QS).

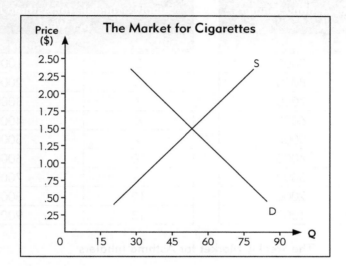

**b** Referring to your graph above, fully explain the consequences of a minimum price control on the market for cigarettes. Include the following in your explanation:
- quantity demanded before AND after the minimum price control
- quantity supplied before AND after the minimum price control
- a problem the minimum price control might create
- a possible solution for the above problem.

_____

_____

_____

_____

_____

_____

_____

_____

_____

_____

_____

_____

_____

ISBN: 9780170241946

_____

_____

_____

_____

_____

_____

_____

_____

Page 147 **52** Use the following supply and demand schedules to construct the market for asthma inhalers.

| Demand Schedule for Asthma Inhalers, per Week | |
|---|---|
| Price ($) | Quantity demanded |
| 5 | 9000 |
| 6 | 8000 |
| 7 | 7000 |
| 8 | 6000 |
| 9 | 5000 |
| 10 | 4000 |
| 11 | 3000 |
| 12 | 2000 |
| 13 | 1000 |

| Supply Schedule for Asthma Inhalers, per Week | |
|---|---|
| Price ($) | Quantity supplied |
| 5 | 1000 |
| 6 | 2000 |
| 7 | 3000 |
| 8 | 4000 |
| 9 | 5000 |
| 10 | 6000 |
| 11 | 7000 |
| 12 | 8000 |
| 13 | 9000 |

**The Weekly Market for Asthma Inhalers**

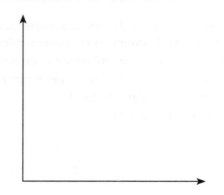

**53** Show the effect of a subsidy ($3) on your diagram.

**54** Fully label your graph using standard notation to illustrate the effect of the subsidy.

**55** Identify the price paid by consumers and the price received by producers.

**56** Explain why these two prices are different.

_____

_____

_____

ISBN: 9780170241946

**57** Use the following demand and supply schedules to construct the market for vitamin tablets..

| Demand Schedule for Vitamin Supplements | |
|---|---|
| Price ($) | Q (000 bottles) |
| 15 | 18 |
| 16 | 15 |
| 17 | 13 |
| 18 | 12 |
| 19 | 10 |
| 20 | 7 |

| Supply Schedule for Vitamin Supplements | |
|---|---|
| Price ($) | Q (000 bottles) |
| 15 | 4 |
| 16 | 8 |
| 17 | 13 |
| 18 | 16 |
| 19 | 19 |
| 20 | 22 |

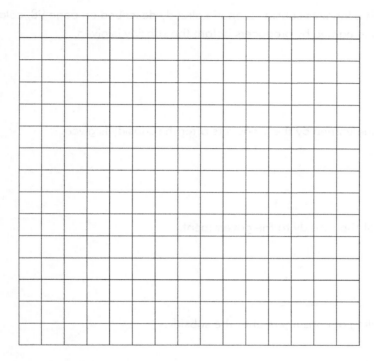

**58** Show the effect of a $2 subsidy on the market for vitamin supplements on your diagram.

**59** Fully label your graph using standard notation to illustrate the effect of the subsidy.

**60** Identify the price paid by consumers and the price received by producers.

**61** Explain why these two prices are different.

_____

_____

_____

**62** List as many goods or services as you can that you think are merit goods.

Page 148

|  |  |  |
|---|---|---|
|  |  |  |
|  |  |  |
|  |  |  |

ISBN: 9780170241946

**4**

**63** Choose two goods or services from your list and outline how the government tries to encourage consumers to use them.

_____

_____

_____

_____

_____

**64** Using the asthma inhalers subsidy scenario already described on page 98, calculate:

**a** Total revenue earned by producers before the subsidy is given.

$ _____

**b** Total revenue earned by the producers after the subsidy is given.

$ _____

**c** Total cost of the subsidy to the government.

$ _____

**d** Total spending of consumers after the subsidy.

$ _____

**65** Using the vitamin supplements subsidy scenario already described on page 99, calculate:

**a** Total revenue earned by producers before the subsidy is given.

$ _____

**b** Total revenue earned by the producers after the subsidy is given.

$ _____

**c** Total cost of the subsidy to the government.

$ _____

ISBN: 9780170241946

**d** Total spending of consumers after the subsidy.

$ _____

**66** Use the following supply and demand schedules to construct a market diagram.

Page 153

| Demand Schedule for High Fat Confectionery, per week | |
|---|---|
| Price ($) | Quantity demanded |
| 1 | 9000 |
| 2 | 8000 |
| 3 | 7000 |
| 4 | 6000 |
| 5 | 5000 |
| 6 | 4000 |
| 7 | 3000 |
| 8 | 2000 |
| 9 | 1000 |

| Supply Schedule for High Fat Confectionery, per week | |
|---|---|
| Price ($) | Quantity supplied |
| 1 | 1000 |
| 2 | 2000 |
| 3 | 3000 |
| 4 | 4000 |
| 5 | 5000 |
| 6 | 6000 |
| 7 | 7000 |
| 8 | 8000 |
| 9 | 9000 |

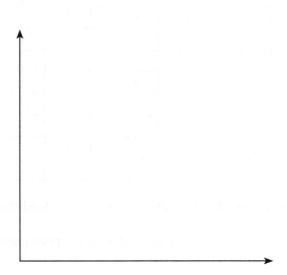

**67** Show the effect of a sales tax ($2) on your diagram.

**68** Fully label your graph using standard notation to identify the price paid by consumers and the price received by producers.

**69** Identify the size of the sales tax on your diagram using a double headed arrow and label.

**70** Explain why these two prices are different.

_____

_____

_____

**71** Use the following demand and supply schedules to construct the market for deep fried cheesecakes.

| Demand Schedule for Deep Fried Cheesecakes | |
| --- | --- |
| P ($) | Q (cheesecake) |
| 4.50 | 100 |
| 5.50 | 80 |
| 6.50 | 60 |
| 7.50 | 40 |
| 8.50 | 20 |
| 9.50 | 10 |

| Supply Schedule for Deep Fried Cheesecakes | |
| --- | --- |
| P ($) | Q (cheesecake) |
| 4.50 | 15 |
| 5.50 | 30 |
| 6.50 | 60 |
| 7.50 | 90 |
| 8.50 | 110 |
| 9.50 | 130 |

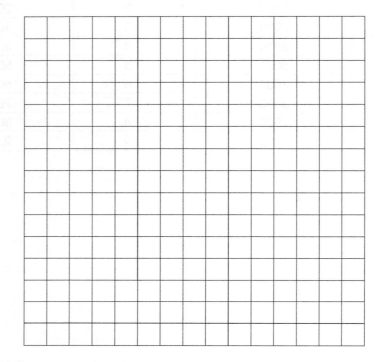

**72** Show the effect of a sales tax of $2.50 on the market for deep fried cheesecakes on your diagram.

**73** Fully label your graph using standard notation to identify the price paid by consumers and the price received by producers.

**74** Explain why these two prices are different.

_____

_____

_____

**75** Identify the size of the sales tax on your diagram using a double headed arrow and label.

Page 153–155
**76** Using the high fat confectionery scenario already described on page 101, calculate:
   **a** Total revenue earned by producers *before* the sales tax.

$ _____

ISBN: 9780170241946

**b**  Total revenue earned by the producers *after* the sales tax.

$ _____

**c**  Total revenue of the sales tax paid to the government.

$ _____

**d**  Total spending of consumers *after* the sales tax.

$ _____

**77**  Using the deep fried cheesecake scenario already described on page 102, calculate:

**a**  Total revenue earned by producers *before* the sales tax.

$ _____

**b**  Total revenue earned by the producers *after* the sales tax.

$ _____

**c**  Total revenue of the sales tax paid to the government.

$ _____

**d**  Total spending of consumers *after* the sales tax.

$ _____

**78**  Define a merit good.

_____

_____

_____

**79**  Define a demerit good.

_____

_____

_____

**80**  List as many goods or services as you can that you think are demerit goods.

| | | |
|---|---|---|
| | | |
| | | |
| | | |
| | | |

**81** Choose two goods or services from your list and outline how the government tries to discourage consumers from using them.

_____

_____

_____

**82** Classify the following as either a merit or demerit good:

|   |   | Merit good | Demerit good |
|---|---|---|---|
| a | Seatbelts | | |
| b | Lead petrol | | |
| c | Cigarettes | | |
| d | Cycle helmets | | |
| e | Literacy | | |
| f | Doctor's visits | | |
| g | Vaccinations | | |
| h | Education | | |
| i | Alcohol | | |
| j | Fruit and vegetables | | |
| k | Illicit drugs | | |

**83** Plot the market for calcium-enriched milk on a graph and use it to answer the questions that follow.

| Market Demand Schedule for Calcium-enriched Milk, per week | |
|---|---|
| Price ($) | Quantity (000 litres) |
| 2.00 | 100 |
| 1.90 | 110 |
| 1.80 | 120 |
| 1.70 | 130 |
| 1.60 | 140 |
| 1.50 | 150 |
| 1.40 | 160 |

| Market Supply Schedule for Calcium-enriched Milk, per week | |
|---|---|
| Price ($) | Quantity (000 litres) |
| 2.00 | 160 |
| 1.90 | 150 |
| 1.80 | 140 |
| 1.70 | 130 |
| 1.60 | 120 |
| 1.50 | 110 |
| 1.40 | 100 |

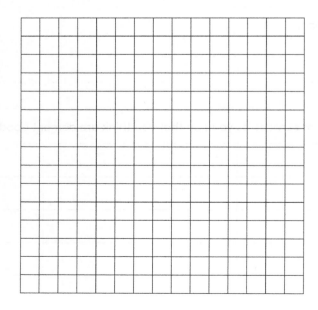

ISBN: 9780170241946

**a** Show the effect of the government imposing a $0.30 subsidy.

**b** Describe what has happened to equilibrium price and quantity.

_____

_____

_____

**c** Calculate the following:

   **i**   Total producer revenue _before_ the subsidy was imposed.

      $ _____

   **ii**  Total producer revenue _after_ the subsidy was imposed.

      $ _____

   **iii** Total cost of the subsidy to the government.

      $ _____

   **iv**  Total consumer expenditure _before_ the subsidy was imposed.

      $ _____

   **v**   Total consumer expenditure _after_ the subsidy was imposed.

      $ _____

   **vi**  The percentage change in total producer revenue.

      _____ %

   **vii** The percentage change in consumer expenditure.

      _____ %

**d** Explain why the government would pay a subsidy.

_____

_____

_____

_____

ISBN: 9780170241946

**4**

e   Explain the relationship between total producer revenue after the subsidy, government spending on the subsidy, and consumer expenditure.

_____

_____

_____

**84** Plot the market for tobacco on a graph and use it to answer the questions that follow.

| Market Demand Schedule for Tobacco, per week | |
|---|---|
| Price ($) | Quantity (000 packets) |
| 12 | 200 |
| 11 | 210 |
| 10 | 220 |
| 9 | 230 |
| 8 | 240 |
| 7 | 250 |
| 6 | 260 |

| Market Supply Schedule for Tobacco, per week | |
|---|---|
| Price ($) | Quantity (000 packets) |
| 12 | 260 |
| 11 | 250 |
| 10 | 240 |
| 9 | 230 |
| 8 | 220 |
| 7 | 210 |
| 6 | 200 |

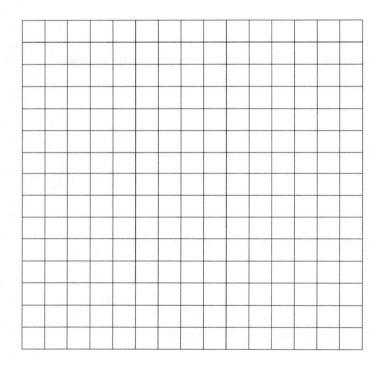

a   Show the effect of the government imposing a $3 tax.

b   Describe what has happened to equilibrium price and quantity.

c   Calculate the following:

   i   Total producer revenue before the tax was imposed.

$ _____

ISBN: 9780170241946

**ii** Total producer revenue after the tax was imposed.

$ _____

**iii** The total revenue collected by the government.

$ _____

**iv** Total consumer expenditure *before* the tax was imposed.

$ _____

**v** Total consumer expenditure *after* the tax was imposed.

$ _____

**vi** The percentage change in total producer revenue.

_____ %

**vii** The percentage change in consumer expenditure.

_____ %

**d** Explain why the government would impose an indirect tax.

_____

_____

_____

_____

**e** Explain the relationship between producers' total revenue after the tax, government revenue from the tax, and consumer expenditure.

_____

_____

_____

**85** Explain why taxes and subsidies are more successful than price minimums and price maximums.

_____

_____

_____

_____

ISBN: 9780170241946

**86** The following graph shows the effect of a sales tax on a market. Identify the areas on the graph;

   **a**  total revenue for producers before the tax was imposed _____

   **b**  total revenue for producers after the tax was imposed _____

   **c**  total revenue collected by the government

   **d**  total consumer expenditure before the tax was imposed _____

   **e**  total consumer expenditure after the tax was imposed _____

   **f**  amount of the tax per unit _____

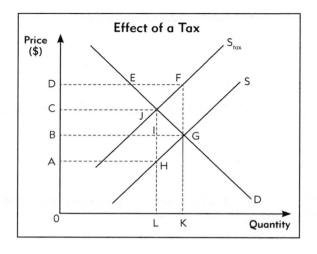

**87** The following graph shows the effect of a subsidy on a market. Identify the areas on the graph;

   **a**  total revenue for producers before the subsidy was paid _____

   **b**  total revenue for producers after the subsidy was paid _____

   **c**  total spending by the government _____

   **d**  total consumer expenditure before the subsidy was paid _____

   **e**  total consumer expenditure after the subsidy was paid _____

   **f**  amount of the subsidy per unit _____

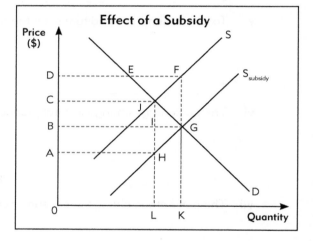

**88** A sales tax will create a new equilibrium price and quantity. Explain how a market will move from the old equilibrium to the new equilibrium.

_____

_____

_____

_____

_____

_____

_____

_____

**89** A subsidy will create a new equilibrium price and quantity. Explain how a market will move from the old equilibrium to the new equilibrium.

_____

_____

_____

ISBN: 9780170241946

**4**

_____

_____

_____

_____

_____

**90** The government is increasing the sales tax on alcohol.

Page 157

   **a** Draw a fully labelled market graph illustrating the market for alcohol, including the increase in sales tax.

   **b** Use the supply and demand model to fully explain how a sales tax would affect (i) suppliers of alcohol, and (ii) the government.

_____

_____

_____

_____

_____

_____

_____

_____

_____

_____

_____

**91** The government is introducing a subsidy on primary school reading books.

   **a**  Draw a fully labelled market graph illustrating the market for primary school reading books showing the introduced subsidy.

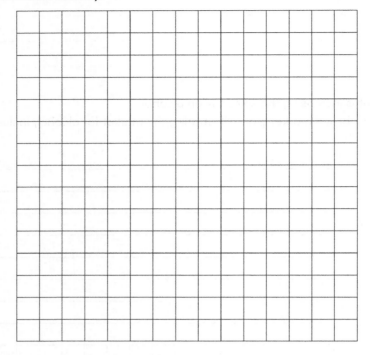

   **b**  Use the supply and demand model to fully explain how a subsidy would affect (i) suppliers of primary school reading books, and (ii) the government.

_____

_____

_____

_____

_____

_____

_____

_____

_____

_____

_____

_____

_____

_____

_____

_____

_____

_____

ISBN: 9780170241946

**92** Discuss how a tax on new cars would affect society. In your answer, you should:
- explain the change in price to the consumer
- explain the change in price to the producer
- fully explain the effect on the government
- explain any benefit to society.

_____

_____

_____

_____

_____

_____

_____

_____

_____

_____

**93** Discuss how a subsidy on bread with added flouride would affect society. In your answer, you should:
- explain the change in price to the consumer
- explain the change in price to the producer
- fully explain the effect on the government
- explain any benefit to society.

_____

_____

_____

_____

_____

_____

_____

_____

_____

_____

_____

_____

_____

ISBN: 9780170241946

# 5 Interdependence of sectors in the New Zealand economy

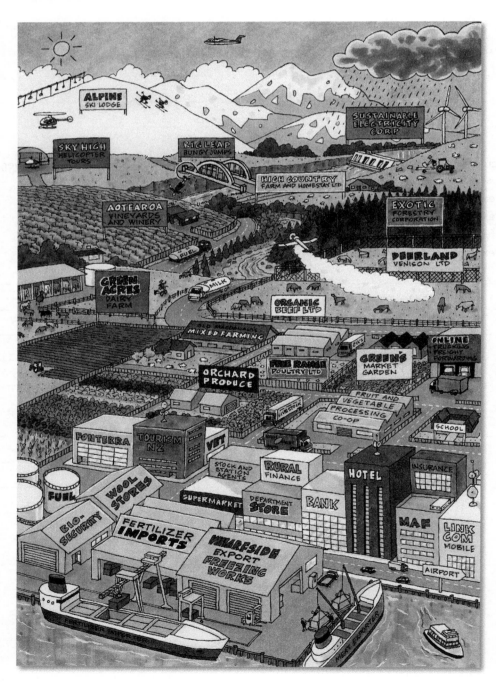

ISBN: 9780170241946

# Interdependence of sectors in the New Zealand economy

**5**

Page 166

1   Using the picture resource on the previous page, identify all primary, all secondary and all tertiary sector producers.

| Primary | Secondary | Tertiary |
|---------|-----------|----------|
|         |           |          |
|         |           |          |
|         |           |          |
|         |           |          |
|         |           |          |

2   Fully explain how the following pairs of firms are interdependent.

a   *Pennycook Accountants* and *Vila Fisheries*.

_____

_____

_____

b   *Dylan's Fruit Shop* and *Issie's Fresh Fruit Orchard*.

_____

_____

_____

c   *Joe's Tannery* and *Gus' Beef Farm*.

_____

_____

_____

d   *Eddie's Fish and Chip Shop* and *Tukaha's Potato Processing Factory*.

_____

_____

_____

3   Using examples, explain the difference between dependence, independence and interdependence.

_____

_____

_____

_____

_____

_____

**4** Give three different and specific examples of a service the tertiary sector provides to each of the following:

**a** A horticulturist.

_____

_____

_____

**b** A mining company.

_____

_____

_____

**c** A farmer.

_____

_____

_____

**d** A car manufacturer.

_____

_____

_____

**5** Draw a simple flow chart of the production process, highlighting the interdependence between the sectors, for each of the following goods and services.

**a** Bread.

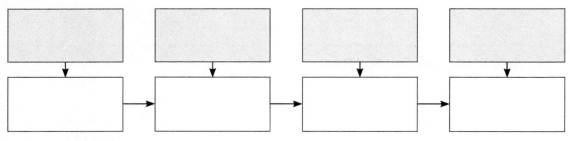

**b** Education.

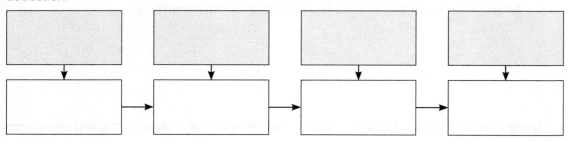

**c** A hamburger.

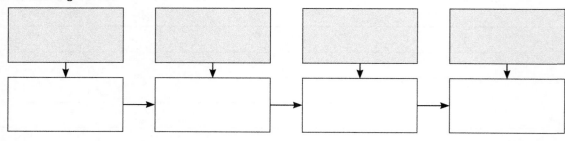

ISBN: 9780170241946

**5**

**6** Give examples of the types of services produced by each of the tertiary service providers below.

| Finance | Accounting | Transportation |
|---|---|---|
|  |  |  |

**7** Describe what is meant by each of these terms:

Page 168

- labour

_____

_____

- land

_____

_____

- capital

_____

_____

- entrepreneurship

_____

_____

**8** Complete the table below to identify the main factor of production (resource) in each scenario. The first example has been done for you.

|   |   | Labour | Land | Capital | Entrepreneurship |
|---|---|---|---|---|---|
| a | Tractors, fences and combine harvesters on a farm |  |  | X |  |
| b | Nurses, doctors and physiotherapists at a hospital |  |  |  |  |
| c | Orange roughy fish stocks |  |  |  |  |
| d | Graeme Hart, owner of *Reynolds Packaging Group* (RPG) |  |  |  |  |
| e | Vats, trucks and bottles at a winery |  |  |  |  |
| f | Carpenters, electricians and plumbers working on site |  |  |  |  |
| g | Sam Morgan, developer of *TradeMe* |  |  |  |  |

ISBN: 9780170241946

9  'Households own all resources.' Explain how this is true.

_____

_____

_____

Page 169

10 Explain the difference between a real flow and a money flow.

_____

_____

_____

11 Complete the table below.

| Real flow | Money flow |
|---|---|
| Goods and services | |
| Resources | |

12 Draw a fully labelled two sector circular flow model showing both real flows and money flows.

13 State the reward or type of income that is linked to each of the following resources.

| Resource | Income/Return |
|---|---|
| Land | |
| Labour | |
| Capital | |
| Entrepreneur | |

ISBN: 9780170241946

**5**

Page 171

14 Complete the following table. All questions refer to a two sector circular flow model. The first example has been done for you.

| | Scenario | Directly affects ... (which flow) | Impact on ... (which sector) | This sector responds by ... | This affects ... (which flow) | Which impacts on ... (which sector) | This sector responds by ... |
|---|---|---|---|---|---|---|---|
| | Unemployment rises | Payments for resources | Households | Decreasing household spending on goods and services | Household spending on goods and services | Firms | Reduced spending on resources by: Reducing production Cutting workers' hours Laying off workers |
| 1 | Signs NZ coming out of recession – household spending up at Christmas | | | | | | |
| 2 | Job losses at the local mill | | | | | | |
| 3 | Unemployment figures down for first time since global financial crisis | | | | | | |
| 4 | Households tightening their belts as winter arrives | | | | | | |

ISBN: 9780170241946

15    Complete the following table.

Page 174

| | Scenario | Directly affects ... (which flow) | Impact on ... (which sector) | This sector responds by ... | This affects ... (which flow) | Which impacts on ... (which sector) | This sector responds by ... |
|---|---|---|---|---|---|---|---|
| | Banks curtain loans to business | Investment | Firms | Reducing spending on resources by: Reducing production Cutting workers' hours Laying off workers | Payment for resources | Households | Decreasing household spending on goods and services AND/OR decreasing savings |
| 1 | Households follow government advice and put money aside for retirement | | | | | | |
| 2 | Highest levels of unemployment yet recorded following global financial meltdown | | | | | | |
| 3 | Unemployment figures down for first time since global financial crisis | | | | | | |
| 4 | Banks announce increased interest rates on business lending | | | | | | |

ISBN: 9780170241946

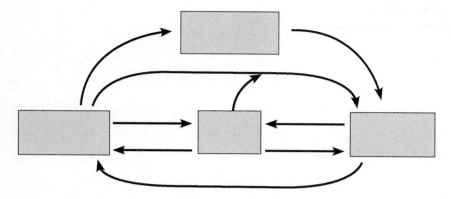

**16** Fully label the four sector circular flow model.

**17** The circular flow diagram below shows economic activity and the relationships between sectors of the economy. Only money flows are shown. Study the diagram to answer the questions that follow.

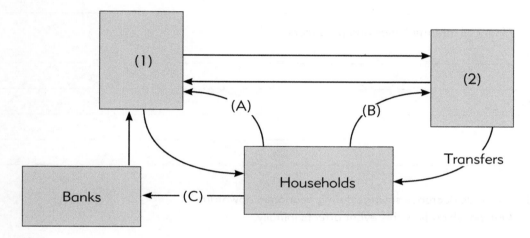

**a** Identify the sectors of the economy labelled:

(1) _____

(2) _____

**b** Identify the money flows labelled:

(A) _____

(B) _____

(C) _____

**c** State the real flow that is linked with the following money flows:

(A) _____

**d** Explain the interdependence that exists between sectors (1) and (2).

_____

_____

_____

_____

_____

**5**

Page 178

**18** For each of the pairs of sectors below explain how they are independent. Include a specific example of this interdependence.

   **a** Households and producers.

   _____

   _____

   _____

   _____

   **b** Government and households.

   _____

   _____

   _____

   _____

   **c** Financial intermediaries and producers.

   _____

   _____

   _____

   _____

   _____

**19** 'Households decrease savings during economic downturn.'

   **a** Outline which flow this event affects initially.

   _____

   **b** Fully explain the impact that 'households decrease savings' has on the financial sector.

   _____

   _____

   _____

   **c** Fully explain the possible flow-on effect this has on firms.

   _____

   _____

   _____

   **d** Fully explain the possible flow-on effect this has on the government.

   _____

   _____

   _____

**20** 'The government increases spending on infrastructure to try to stimulate the economy.'

   **a** Outline which flow this event affects initially.

   _____

ISBN: 9780170241946

**b**  Fully explain the impact that 'government increases spending' has on households.

_____

_____

_____

**c**  Fully explain the possible flow-on effect this has on the financial sector.

_____

_____

_____

**d**  Fully explain the possible flow-on effect this has on the government.

_____

_____

_____

**21**  Identify all withdrawals and injections into the three sector circular flow model.

| Withdrawals | Injections |
| --- | --- |
|  |  |
|  |  |
|  |  |

**22**  The diagram below shows two sectors of the economy and the money flows between them.

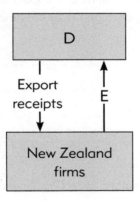

**i**  Name the sector labelled D in the diagram above.

_____

**ii**  Name the money flow labelled E in the diagram above.

_____

**iii**  State an example of an export receipt.

_____

Page 180

**23** Complete the table below.

| Scenario | | Increases payments | | Export receipts | |
|---|---|---|---|---|---|
| | | Increase | Decrease | Increase | Decrease |
| 1 | The Rugby World Cup (RWC) sees thousands of tourists coming to New Zealand | | | | |
| 2 | A fall in the number of Japanese car imports | | | | |
| 3 | An increase in New Zealand purchases of the latest computer product | | | | |
| 4 | Global crisis sees a fall in New Zealand logs being sent to Asia | | | | |
| 5 | New Zealanders going to Gallipoli to remember ANZAC Day reaches record numbers | | | | |
| 6 | Weta Digital is hired to create special effects on another US blockbuster | | | | |

**24** Explain how an increase in transfer payments may affect the overseas sector.

_____

_____

_____

_____

_____

Page 183

**25** For each of the scenarios listed below, outline one impact on the sector identified in brackets.

**a** Tourist dissatisfaction with Europe's high prices sees increased numbers of travellers to New Zealand (Producers).

_____

_____

_____

_____

**b** The US relaxes tariffs on New Zealand steel (Producers).

_____

_____

_____

_____

**c** OCR (interest rates) rise (Households).

_____

_____

_____

_____

ISBN: 9780170241946

**d** New employment legislation sees workers incomes fall (Households).

_____

_____

_____

_____

_____

**e** A loosening of the government purse strings sees social welfare spending increase (Households).

_____

_____

_____

_____

**26** For each scenario above outline the flow-on effects for at least two other sectors.

**a** **i** Sector: _____

_____

_____

_____

_____

_____

**ii** Sector: _____

_____

_____

_____

_____

_____

**b** **i** Sector: _____

_____

_____

_____

_____

_____

**ii** Sector: _____

_____

_____

_____

_____

_____

ISBN: 9780170241946

**5**

**c** **i** Sector: _____

_____

_____

_____

_____

**ii** Sector: _____

_____

_____

_____

_____

**d** **i** Sector: _____

_____

_____

_____

_____

**ii** Sector: _____

_____

_____

_____

_____

**e** **i** Sector: _____

_____

_____

_____

_____

**ii** Sector: _____

_____

_____

_____

_____

ISBN: 9780170241946

**27** Complete the five sector circular flow model (ensure your arrows are pointing the right way).

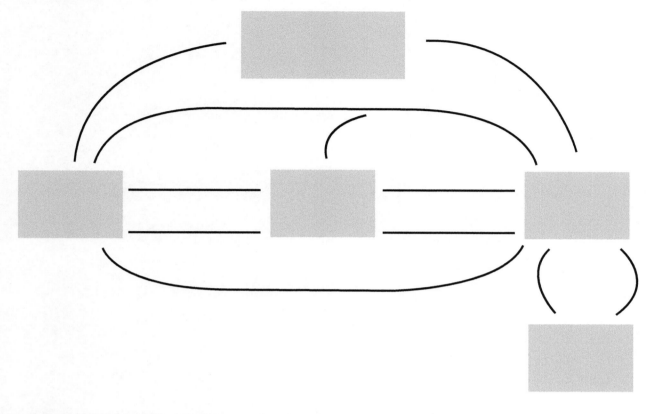

**28** Explain how an increased withdrawal affects economic activity, referring to the circular flow model in your answer.

_____
_____
_____
_____
_____
_____
_____
_____

**29** Explain how an increased injection affects economic activity, referring to the circular flow model in your answer.

_____
_____
_____
_____
_____
_____
_____
_____
_____

ISBN: 9780170241946

NELSON
CENGAGE Learning·

**Eco1 PLUS Activities for NCEA Economics Level One**
**1st Edition**
**Anne Younger**
**Kelly Bigwood**

Cover designer: Cheryl Rowe
Text designer: Book Design
Production controller: Siew Han Ong
Reprint: Jennifer Foo

Any URLs contained in this publication were checked for currency during the production process. Note, however, that the publisher cannot vouch for the ongoing currency of URLs.

For product information and technology assistance,
in Australia call **1300 790 853**;
in New Zealand call **0800 449 725**

For permission to use material from this text or product, please email
**aust.permissions@cengage.com**

**National Library of New Zealand Cataloguing-in-Publication Data**
National Library of New Zealand Cataloguing-in-Publication Data

Younger, Anne.
Eco1 plus / Anne Younger.
ISBN 978-017024-194-6
1. Economics. 2. Economics—Problems, exercises, etc.
I. Title.
330.076—dc 23

**Cengage Learning Australia**
Level 7, 80 Dorcas Street
South Melbourne, Victoria Australia 3205

**Cengage Learning New Zealand**
Unit 4B Rosedale Office Park
331 Rosedale Road, Albany, North Shore 0632, NZ

For learning solutions, visit **cengage.com.au**

Printed in Australia by Ligare Pty Limited
2 3 4 5 6 7 8 22 21 20 19 18

## Eco 1 Plus
## Activities for NCEA
## Economics Level One

*Eco 1 PLUS* covers all that is needed to attain NCEA Level 1 Economics. This workbook is highly suitable for independent learners who wish to be fully prepared for the new achievement standards.

- Supports the textbook *Eco 1* – provides spaces for student activities including pre-drawn graphs and diagrams.

- Contains extra questions in a range of styles for valuable practice of Economics concepts and skills.

- Targets the new achievement standard requirements – Achieved, Merit and Excellence.

- Excellent for class use and homework.

- An ideal resource for revision ahead of examinations.

### ABOUT THE AUTHORS
**Anne Younger**
- Currently teaching senior Economics at ACG NZIC Auckland.
- Author of *Eco 1 – Economics for NCEA Level One*, *Eco 2 – Economics for NCEA Level Two* and *Eco2Plus*.
- Previous teaching experience at the Faculty of Education – The University of Auckland, Birkenhead College, Rangitoto College and Diocesan School for Girls.
- Involvement in external examination marking, national moderation and seminar presentations in Economics.

**Kelly Bigwood**
- Currently teaching preservice teachers at the Faculty of Education, The University of Auckland.
- Co-author of *Eco 1 – Economics for NCEA Level One*, *Pathfinder Year 11 Economics*, *Consumer Economics Book A* and *Consumer Economics Book B*.
- Previous teaching experience at Pakuranga College, Mount Roskill Grammar School and Auckland Girls' Grammar School.
- Involvement in external examination marking, national moderation and seminar presentations in Economics.

NELSON
CENGAGE Learning™
For learning solutions, visit **cengage.com.au**

ISBN 978-0170241946

9 780170 241946